Kevin has a heart for people in ministry. And he writes as one who knows.

—John Ortberg, Pastor and Author, Menlo Park Presbyterian Church

The last few decades have shouted loud and clear that sustainable leadership in the church requires a healthy leader. Kevin Harney makes the diagnosis and then prescribes a good and attainable plan.

—Randy Frazee, Teaching Pastor, Willow Creek Community Church

In a sea of leadership books, this one stands out because it addresses the critical topic of the inner life of a leader. Kevin has been a friend and partner in ministry for many years. I know his track record as a leader. I encourage church leaders to read this book carefully and allow God to transform them on the inside so they can experience a lifetime of fruitful ministry on the outside.

—Lee Strobel, author of *The Case for the Real Jesus*

There is the ring of authenticity to what Kevin Harney writes about leadership because it is backed by his track record as an effective Christian leader and as a loving and devoted husband and father.

—Ajith Fernando, National Director, Youth for Christ, Sri Lanka

If Christian leaders will prayerfully absorb *Leadership from the Inside Out*, I am confident that they will emerge with a fortified soul, more in love with their God, more aware of their own heart, more settled in their calling, and more passionate about loving others. If you want to be in ministry two decades from now, you will be well served by reading this practical book.

—Gary Thomas, author of *Sacred Marriage* and *Sacred Parenting*

In this wonderful book, Kevin Harney helped me to see that outside my inside is the world I'm called to change, and inside my outside is where I find the Savior who has called me to leadership. If only I will allow him to make my inside life consistent with my outside life, then maybe I can get on with turning the world upside down.

—Calvin Miller, author of *The Sermon Maker*

Leadership from the Inside Out is an outstanding resource for every church leadership team. Lock arms and trek through this book together! Kevin Harney masterfully communicates how to examine the inner life to sustain leadership for the long run.

—Nancy Grisham, PhD, Evangelism Leader,
Livin' Ignited

As I read Kevin's book, I found my heart beating faster. It was beating faster because it was so real, practical, and insightful. This is a must-read for all leaders.

—Bob Bouwer, Senior Pastor, Faith Church, Dyer, IN

In this frank, open, practical, and hard-hitting book, Kevin Harney deals with what is today hands-down the most urgently needed yet most neglected aspect of church and mission leadership: the personal, psycho-emotional, and spiritual inner being of the leader. This is the best book on the subject I've ever seen.

—Charles Van Engen, Arthur F. Glasser Professor of
Biblical Theology of Mission, Fuller Theological Seminary

leadership

from the

inside out

leadership
from the
inside out

Examining the Inner Life of a Healthy Church Leader

Kevin Harney

ZONDERVAN.com/
AUTHORTRACKER
follow your favorite authors

Leadership from the Inside Out
Copyright © 2007 by Kevin Harney

Requests for information should be addressed to:

Zondervan, *Grand Rapids, Michigan 49530*

Library of Congress Cataloging-in-Publication Data

Harney, Kevin.
    Leadership from the inside out : examining the inner life of a healthy church
leader / Kevin Harney.
        p. cm. – (The leadership network innovation series)
    Includes bibliographical references.
    ISBN-13: 978-0-310-25943-5
    ISBN-10: 0-310-25943-6
    1. Christian leadership. I. Title.
BV652.1.H245 2007
253 – dc22
                                                                    2007026426

Interior design by Matthew Van Zomeren

Printed in the United States of America

07 08 09 10 11 12 • 15 14 13 12 11 10 9 8 7 6 5 4 3 2 1

*To the leaders God has graciously placed in my life who have
"fought the good fight, finished the race, and kept the faith."*

*I know you are cheering for the next generation of leaders
to whom you have passed the baton.*

Well done, good and faithful servants!

Contents

Acknowledgments

I am humbled by the number of people God has placed in my life to shape me as a leader. Their example, love for God, and passion for the church formed what is helpful in these pages. I give heartfelt thanks to:

The lead staff of Corinth Reformed Church for their friendship and faithfulness over fourteen years of partnership in ministry: Don, Deb, Barb, Ryan, Kevin, Mike, Doug, and all those on the Corinth staff who have served so faithfully.

The senior pastors who have been my bosses and teachers: Mel, Rich, Henry, Ron, and Don. Your example has shaped my leadership life.

The members of my pastors small group: Todd, Tim M., Dave, Brian, Tim V., Jim, and James. You have become like brothers to me, and some of you have watched my back for almost a decade.

The members of my "large-church pastors" group: Jeff, Jim P., Bill, Mike, Tom, Jim L., and Don. Your wisdom and passion for the kingdom have sharpened me as a leader.

The pastors and leaders who have become friends over the years: Bob, Paul H., Chris, Paul B., Wayne, Brad, Adam, Ryan, Josh, Mark, Lee, Nancy, Randy, Charlie, Ken, Howie, Dave, Michelle, and many others. You have made me a better leader than I could ever have been on my own.

To the membership and rules committee of the CCH: Ron, Brad, Gary, and Harold. Your wisdom and counsel have helped direct my life on many occasions.

To my wife, Sherry, and my sons, Zach, Josh, and Nate. No one knows and sees my "inner life" more than you do. You have cheered me on when I have been a faithful leader, and extended amazing grace when I have fallen on my face. I love each of you and appreciate how God has formed my leadership through our life together.

Introduction

The Life-Giving Power
of Self-Examination

I am not easily given to tears. But this day they flowed freely.

I was caught off guard. Honestly, I didn't see it coming.

Josh, my middle son, was working on a video project. As he sorted through hours of tape, he came across a moment captured almost a decade earlier. On the back deck of our home were four couples and their children. The sun was shining, smiles were on every face, kids were splashing in the pool, laughter filled the air.

It was a good day.

Years before this day was recorded on video, the eight of us had been part of the same congregation on the West Coast. We had ministered together in this church, crawling through the same foxholes and working tirelessly to build a biblical community that reached into the world with God's love. Through our common journey, God had bound our hearts together. We loved each other. We were family.

After years of service together, we had all wound up going our separate ways. But eventually, by a delightful twist of God's hand, we all came to be ministering and serving God in the Midwest, living within a couple of hours of each other, about two thousand miles from where we first had met. And so we got together at our house to reunite.

As I watched the scene unfold, I was surprised by the tears that ran down my cheeks. I remembered our conversations that day, the visions we shared, and our celebration of life. All of the adults on our back deck were gifted leaders; each one loved Jesus with a fervent heart. All of the eleven kids splashing in the pool were being raised in loving homes and were enfolded in churches that were feeding their souls and shaping their hearts.

If you had come to me later that evening, after everyone had gone home, and asked, "Where will these four couples be a decade from now?" I would have answered confidently, "I believe each of these couples, Sherry and I included, will be happily married, serving faithfully, leading boldly, and raising their children to love and walk with Jesus."

What shattered my heart as I watched that decade-old video time capsule was that three of the couples are now divorced. By God's grace, Sherry and I are still together and serving the Lord, but all three of the other couples are no longer married. Unbeknownst to all of us that day, eight of those smiling and joy-filled children would in their adolescent years face the challenges that come in the aftermath of divorce. As I watched the tape of that glorious day, my heart was broken.

I wondered what had happened and reflected on what might have been.

I don't write this to be critical of these friends. Sherry and I still care deeply about each of them. I recount this moment because I don't believe any of these couples wanted things to end the way they did. There was a time when they loved each other. There was a season when they served joyfully as partners in ministry. All were leaders. All bore great fruit. All had enormous kingdom potential. All dreamed great dreams for God.

As I viewed the video, I found myself reflecting on the reality that so many gifted and passionate leaders hit obstacles along their journeys and stumble. I've thought long and hard about why so many who start the race strongly don't finish well. What has come to my heart again and again is that the problem lies in the leader's inner life. So many leaders have developed great skills, attended excellent conferences, read powerful books, and sharpened their management abilities. But something goes wrong on the inside. Few leaders drop out of ministry because they lack the skills. Instead, too often they lack an examined inner life shaped by the Holy Spirit. This vacancy leads to actions and decisions that compromise their ministries, damage their relationships, and undermine their integrity. They are not bad leaders or bad people; they simply forget to live an examined life. And when the inner life is left to erode to a critical point, the outer world implodes.

Leaders today seek to serve in the wake of the countless moral failings, financial misdealings, lapses of integrity, and relational explosions of those who have gone before us. It's at our own peril that we press on with mindlessly busy schedules, resistance to accountability, and lifestyles that allow us no time to look into our own souls. We need to lead from the inside out.

Fun in the Sun

We were ignorant.

We were clueless.

We were kids growing up in Orange County, California, and when summer came, we went to Huntington Beach ... all day!

It was a simple and glorious process. Mom would load us into the family station wagon (for younger readers, imagine a minivan smashed down to about half its height), we would throw our surfboards, towels, and beach paraphernalia into the back, and off we'd go. Mom would dump us at the beach for the whole day.

We loved it!

The beach was paradise for prepubescent kids and high-energy adolescents. My memories of those days are vivid and blissful. I can still hear the cries of seagulls as they dive-bombed us for sandwich crusts. I can feel the Pacific Ocean drying on my body. I can taste the saltwater on my lips. I can close my eyes and see the curl of the waves and the glowing orange sun setting over Catalina Island. I can smell the fast food cooking at the Jack-in-the-Box just south of the Huntington Pier, where all of our friends congregated between lifeguard stations three and five.

How was I to know I was putting myself at risk? I had no idea my future health was being compromised.

I was just having fun ... lots of fun!

In the 1960s and '70s, SPF was just a meaningless cluster of consonants. Today, the acronym SPF (sun protection factor) is a familiar reminder that the rays of the sun can severely damage our skin if we don't take precautionary measures. If we want to avoid problems later in life, we learn to slather sunscreen on our skin when we're going to be out in the sun.

In those days, the girls actually put baby oil on their skin to help them tan faster. All of us kids could feel the warmth of the sun baking our skin from the time we arrived in the morning until the cool hours of the evening. Those who surfed got a double dose. During the hours we paddled around and sat on our boards, waiting for the next set of waves, the reflection of sunlight off the water increased our UV consumption.

My mom is a redhead, and she passed on her skin pigmentation to her children. I never really tanned; I just burned. Then I would burn on my burn. Then, as the summer went on, I would burn even more. But because I loved to surf, hang out at the beach, and be with my friends, my three-month sunburn seemed a small price to pay.

Facing the Hard Truth

It started as a small bump on my left cheek. I didn't think much of it—just a blemish that would soon disappear. No big deal.

But after a few weeks, it hadn't gone away. Instead, the tiny bump became more pronounced and turned red. Then it ulcerated and broke open. With time, it healed and then ulcerated again. Since I was in my midthirties, I knew it wasn't an attack of acne.

I called a dermatologist and set a date for a checkup. Dr. Dekkinga examined the skin under my eyebrow and on my cheek. He determined it would be best to perform a biopsy right away and discovered I had a mild form of skin cancer called basal cell carcinoma. We set an appointment for Mohs Micrographic Surgery the next week. When I came in, they numbed my face, cut out the bad spots, and sewed me up. I drove home with a couple of wads of gauze taped to my face and with the sober realization that the damage I did to my skin as a boy was more serious than I ever could have dreamed.

Dr. Dekkinga made it very clear that I would need to see him every six to twelve months—for the rest of my life! Regular professional skin exams would be part of my yearly rhythm whether I liked it or not. And on top of this, my doctor asked me to pay attention to any unusual skin blemishes, sores, or discoloration. In effect, he asked me to become my own physician by learning to recognize problems with my skin before they became serious.

Since I would be seeing Dr. Dekkinga regularly and trusting him with life and death issues, I decided to get to know him on a less clinical basis. We had lunch, talked about life, love for God, and ministry, and have become friends over the years. Dr. Dekkinga (or Jack, as I now call him) has become a wise and trusted friend.

Under his direction, I began a regimen of self-exams. About once a week, I evaluate my skin from head to toe. After about two years of these self-examinations, I found two more spots that concerned me. I called Jack's office and set up a time he could look them over to see if he was concerned.

He was concerned!

After a biopsy, he concluded that I needed two more Mohs procedures. He scheduled the surgery, and we went through the whole process again. Jack carefully drew a circle around the epicenter of each problem on my face. He then carefully cut out the trouble areas. Finally, he sewed up the spots with skillful hands.

Once again, we had gotten to the problem while it was small and circumvented the major issues I might have faced if I had ignored those spots on my skin. My regimen of self-exams had paid off. And you better believe that to this day, I regularly, consistently, and thoroughly examine my skin. If I fail to, it could cost me my life.

Turning Patients into Dermatologists

Jack sipped his coffee and told me about how he became a dermatologist. His uncle, also a skin doctor, had a big impact on him. But what I heard most as I listened to his story was that he loves to help people and that dermatology is his calling, his passion.

As we conversed, I was struck by a recurring theme in his practice. Dr. Dekkinga doesn't simply want to help people once they become ill or have a problem. He is committed to helping them prevent serious skin problems. He wants to be a partner with his patients and invites them into the personal-health process.

He leveled his eyes at me and said, "I can turn patients into excellent dermatologists." I knew immediately what he meant. He wasn't saying he expected his patients to do his job. But he is committed to helping us do our part in maintaining personal health. As he spoke, it struck me that he had been training me, without my knowing it, for a number of years. We had spoken about what my skin looked and felt like before I had come in for a diagnosis. He had exhorted me to call as soon as I saw a problem spot on my skin — or better yet, before I could see it. What wisdom!

I don't plan on going into dermatology professionally, but I can do a fairly good job of identifying basal and squamous cell spots before they pose a significant threat to my health. This skill, taught by a trusted friend, has already spared me more than one surgery.

You might not need to evaluate your skin's health every week like I do, but you do need to regularly reflect on your inner life. Self-examination is essential in the life of every leader. Your personal choices are never just personal; your choices and the condition of your inner life impact others. What you do as a leader, and even your motives, can affect your family, friends, an entire church community. Your life as a leader touches more people than you can imagine.

Who's Watching Your Back?

During one of my checkups, Dr. Dekkinga mentioned that I should have my wife examine the skin on my back. I can't get a close look at my back, but my wife can. It seems obvious, but I had never thought of it. My wife could save my life if she identifies a problem I can't see.

In the same way, leaders need people who can help us identify potential areas of trouble we can't see. In a sense, we need people we love and respect to say, "I've got your back," and really mean it. We must have the courage to invite others to point out problems developing in our lives. This means we need to develop the humility to listen to and learn from those who have a vantage point different from ours. We are wisest when we have relationships and networks that fortify our lives as leaders.

Healthy leaders not only practice self-examination but also move beyond reflection to invite others into the deep parts of their souls. Leaders who withstand the pressures of ministry over time are those who surround themselves with people who will speak the truth in love. The best leaders will ask, even beg, others to show them where they need to grow, where they are broken, where sin lurks in the dark corners of their hearts. Where we have blind spots, those who are close to us, who love us, can identify areas in which we need to repent, change, grow.

An Invitation to Self-Examination

Year after year we watch as highly gifted Christian leaders shipwreck their lives, families, ministries, and businesses. What they lack is an examined and healthy inner life. This is the missing piece in leadership today. Too many leaders spend huge amounts of time and money developing a powerful skill set but forget to nurture and guard their own souls.

As I write this book, I am humbled because I know I am a far cry from being the model of a healthy church leader. I am a frail, broken, and sinful person who depends on the grace of Jesus every day. I have not perfected the ideas in this book. Rather, I write as a fellow traveler on the road to becoming a healthy church leader.

My prayer is that the ideas in this book will help each of us continue in the glorious calling God has placed on our lives. May we echo the apostle Paul's words:

> Not that I have already obtained all this, or have already been made perfect, but I press on to take hold of that for which Christ Jesus took hold of me. Brothers, I do not consider myself yet to have taken hold of it. But one thing I do: Forgetting what is behind and straining toward what is ahead, I press on toward the goal to win the prize for which God has called me heavenward in Christ Jesus.
>
> —Philippians 3:12–14

In this book, I'll use several body parts as an analogy to help us focus on how to practice self-examination in many areas of our lives. We can't cover every area of a leader's life, but I pray that the process of self-examination covered in this book will help you develop a process you can apply to any point of need.

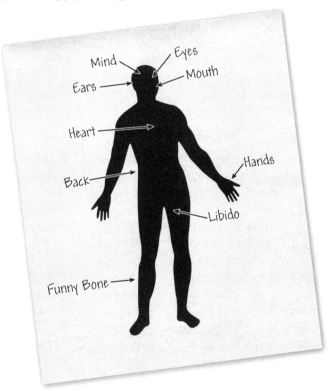

If we walk in wisdom, we can learn to conduct regular self-exams and experience a transformation that will bring joy and health. As you read this book, don't expect a monastic view of soul development that takes you out of the world and focuses only on disciplines like Bible study and prayer. True soul development includes every part of our inner lives — intellectual growth, sexual purity, motives for serving, the need for rest, and much, much more. We need to develop a habit of self-examination that spans the whole of who we are.

The vision of this book is to assist you as you discover the health, wisdom, and joy of leading from the inside out. It also aims to give you tools for self-examination. In addition, it is written to help you discover practical ways you can forge alliances to aid you in living an examined and healthy life.

Forged in the Furnace of Real Ministry

I am a practitioner, not a theorist. I write not from an ivory tower but from the trenches of daily ministry. I have been immersed in church service for almost three decades. I love the local church! With all of its warts and weirdness, it's still the bride of Christ and the best hope for reaching the world with Christ's love and for growing believers to maturity.

Most of the illustrations and commentary in this book grew out of my past thirteen years of ministry in one congregation. Since you will hear a lot about Corinth Church in this book, let me briefly set the context.

I was called to this church in 1993. On my first Sunday, they celebrated their one hundredth year. The church was made up of about 250 people who loved Jesus and had a heart for the world. Their desire was to share God's love with the community, but they were not sure how to go about doing it. So when I committed to lead the church, we agreed that we would do whatever it took to be a church for our community and the world, as long as it did not compromise God's Word. What has staggered me over the years is that they have kept that commitment.

From 1993 to 2007, Corinth Church has transitioned from being exclusively traditional in worship style to having multiple services with many worship styles. We also planted Wayfarer Community Church, and God is impacting many lives through this daughter congregation. I am not a big numbers person, but the growth of the church does tell part of the story. Every number is a life, and God has touched many lives over the years at Corinth. At present, the church ministers to about two thousand people weekly. In 2006, over seventy people made a first-time commitment to Jesus Christ, and they were incorporated into the life of the church. The staff has grown from four people to over thirty (five full-time and the rest part-time). They have added three buildings, which house a worship center that can seat over a thousand (and expand to seat up to two thousand), a children's center, a youth center for high school students and another for junior high students, a new office complex, and adult-education space. Yet through all of this transition, there has been amazing unity in the church. Over 90 percent of those who were part of the church in 1993 are still joyfully connected, serving, and worshiping.

Leadership never functions in a vacuum. This sketch of Corinth Church will give you a picture of the ministry setting that birthed much of what is written in this book. The picture will become clearer as you read on. Your ministry setting is unique and your leadership style grows out of who God has made you to be. But many of the lessons in this book can be adapted to your life and leadership context as the Holy Spirit speaks to your heart.

Help Along the Way

Learning to live an authentic and examined life demands daily choices that are consistent with God's desires for us. To help you take steps in the right direction, you will find the following five tools throughout this book. Each will help you fashion new ways of thinking, living, and relating. They will support you in building an examined life as well as in discovering ways you can invite others to keep you accountable to God's vision for you.

1. *Self-Examination Suggestions.* Throughout this book, you will find sidebars titled "Self-Examination Suggestion," which give ideas for practicing self-examination. These ideas are intended as starting points for reflection as well as for outer action. Use them as a launching pad to develop patterns and disciplines that lead to health and help you avoid pitfalls in ministry. Some of these suggestions will be new to you; others are as old as the church and the Word of God. Through all of them, the Holy Spirit can transform your life.

2. *I've Got Your Back.* Because we can't see every part of our lives clearly, we need people who will cover our backs. We need to establish the habit of inviting others to warn us when we're in harm's way, when our attitudes are poor, and when our actions are dangerous. Because of our sinister ability to rationalize, we need to partner with those who will speak the truth to us and challenge us to take steps to lead lives that honor God. Throughout this book, sidebars titled "I've Got Your Back" will suggest ways to invite others into your life on a new level of intimacy and accountability.

3. *Doctor's Insights.* Wise people get regular medical check-ups to catch health problems before they become critical. Many doctors recommend that their patients consistently practice self-examination to maintain good health. Those who refuse to listen to their doctors do so at their own peril. In the same way, leaders who fail to practice self-examination and who do not allow others to keep them accountable are putting themselves in harm's way. Since doctors know a great deal about the wisdom of regular checkups and preventive care, I interviewed a few to learn from their wisdom. Each of the "Doctor's Insights" sidebars in this book offer thoughts about preventive care for our souls.

4. *Network Building.* We can't lead in isolation. We are wise to build a network of people who will help us lead in ways that honor God and bless others. The "Network Building" sidebars in this book give examples of such networks. These stories are drawn from numerous sources, including the staff and congregation of Corinth Reformed Church, pastors small groups I have been part of, networks of friends, and my family. Though this book is primarily about innovative leadership in the church, the networks we build beyond the church have a great impact on all that we do and on who we become, so I've included examples of these also.

5. *Help from My Friends.* As I wrote this book, I contacted some leaders I respect and trust. First, I asked if

they would share a few thoughts on how they nurture their inner lives so they can stay spiritually healthy. Then I invited them to describe how they create lines of accountability and build networks that strengthen them as they serve Christ and his church. You will find the insights of these wise leaders in the sidebars titled "Help from My Friends."

Also, chapters 1–9 each begin with a brief journal entry. These are not meant to be my thoughts exclusively, though I have felt much of what is recorded in these reflections. They are expressions of what church leaders feel at different times in their lives and ministries. I have had the pleasure to interact with many leaders over the course of my ministry. Through these conversations, I have heard the pain, challenges, and joys leaders experience. These opening words grow out of these interactions, and I hope, as you read them, you will discover an honest expression of things you feel at various times in your ministry.

God is searching for leaders who have the courage to look deeply into their souls and identify areas of danger. He is also longing for leaders to be honest when they have crossed lines and become comfortable living with hidden sin. The Maker of heaven and earth is ready to remake our hearts, restore our souls, and give us new beginnings. He is calling leaders to have the courage and humility to build networks and relationships that are transparent and provide accountability. His eyes are on you and me. With tender and powerful love, he is offering a new way of leading—from the inside out.

chapter 1

Love Strengthens Every Relationship

The Leader's Heart

There are days, weeks, even months that my heartbeat is weak, almost too faint to be heard even by God's spiritual stethoscope. If the truth were known, if people could see inside of me, they would be shocked! In these seasons, I am not inspired by love and a lofty sense of God's calling; I am just grinding through each day trying to get my work done and praying for God to reignite the fire. And I hope that no one will notice I'm one heartbeat from spiritual cardiac arrest. O God, search my heart. Rekindle in me a love for you and for others that will lead me to an inspired, passionate, and fruitful ministry. Strengthen my heart, I pray.

> " 'Love the Lord your God with all your heart and with all your soul and with all your mind and with all your strength.' ... 'Love your neighbor as yourself.' There is no commandment greater than these."
>
> —Mark 12:30–31

> Jesus went through all the towns and villages, teaching in their synagogues, preaching the good news of the kingdom and healing every disease and sickness. When he saw the crowds, he had compassion on them, because they were harassed and helpless, like sheep without a shepherd.
>
> —Matthew 9:35–36

> You will seek me and find me when you seek me with all your heart.
>
> —Jeremiah 29:13

Christmas 2004 was different from any other. Most years of my adult life I celebrated the birth of Jesus with my wife and three sons. Those were glorious times of family gatherings, exchanging gifts, candlelight services, and playing in freshly fallen Michigan snow.

But this year my attention was two thousand miles away. I got on a plane for a rush trip to Orange County. My dad was dying.

The doctors said operating on his heart could kill him. But not operating would be a death sentence. He decided to have surgery, and all of us kids gathered around his hospital bed with him and Mom. We prayed for his heart, for the doctors, for a great work of God in his life, for healing. By God's grace, through faithful prayers, and by the hands of a skilled medical team, my dad made it through the surgery, and his heart became stronger than it had been for many years.

During the winter of 2004, I was confronted by a simple and profound reality. When the heart stops beating, life ends. I always knew this, but it struck me in a new way. As I stood looking at my father lying in a hospital bed, it felt personal.

What's true of our hearts is also true of our spiritual lives and our calling as leaders. If our heart stops beating, we die. Sadly, leaders can mask the reality that their hearts are sick. Sometimes we can even fool ourselves into believing that our hearts are beating strong. It's possible to preach, hold board meetings, lead an organization, and appear to be very much alive long after we have gone through spiritual cardiac arrest. We all have learned that we can go through the motions of leadership with an empty heart. Love is our heartbeat, and too often our heartbeat is weaker than we want to admit.

How is your heart? Is it strong and healthy? Is it weak and faltering? Has it stopped beating altogether?

Symptoms Check
My Heart Is Weak

☐ I minister more out of duty than out of love for God.

☐ I can go days or even weeks without sitting at the feet of Jesus, feeding on his Word, or speaking with him in prayer.

☐ When I prepare messages, my mind is always focused on what others will learn, and the truth of Scripture rarely pierces my heart or stirs my passion.

☐ When I lead in prayer or pray with others, the words sound right to the casual observer, but they feel hollow and empty to me.

☐ I see the people in my church or ministry as a distraction from getting my work done.

☐ I find myself structuring my life in a way that isolates me from people.

☐ I have become so busy doing church work that I leave no time to connect with spiritual seekers.

☐ I can't remember the last time I shed a tear for a lost person.

A Passionate Heart

The question was malicious, fired at Jesus like a bullet. It was a test, not a conversation starter. "Which is the greatest commandment in the Law?" (Matt. 22:36). Jesus responded, "Love the Lord your God with all your heart and with all your soul and with all your mind" (v. 37). Jesus emphasized that every other commandment comes after this one. Until we are seeking to fulfill this calling, we can't do anything effectively.

Help from My Friends
What Do You Do to Stay Connected to God?

Some years ago, I began two very simple practices that have made a big difference in my spiritual life and in the whole feel and flow of my day. First, when I wake up, I roll out of bed onto my knees. I don't let my feet hit the ground, because then I will begin running ahead with all of my tasks for the day. I am a morning person, and when I get going, I can forget to put first things first. So I go straight to my knees and talk with God. This conversation can last thirty seconds, a few minutes, or sometimes longer. I have noticed through the years that this practice has helped me examine my life and keep good tabs on what is really happening in my heart. This simple discipline has become a physical demonstration, at the start of my day, of how I want to live. I long for my heart to be bowed down and for God to be first.

Second, I head to a chair in the study and open my Bible. I spend just a few minutes reading a short passage and meditating on God's Word. I know I will sit there later and spend more time studying the Bible, but this is just a chance to calibrate my heart and mind for the day.

— Sherry Harney, author and speaker

A heart passionately in love with God is the starting point of a healthy life and ministry. This is why Jesus warns the church of Ephesus (and all of God's people to this day), "Yet I hold this against you: You have forsaken your first love. Remember the height from which you have fallen! Repent and do the things you did at first. If you do not repent, I will come to you and remove your lampstand from its place" (Rev. 2:4–5).

When God is no longer our first love, our leadership lives are in danger. When other things, even good things, take supremacy in our hearts, we are in dangerous territory.

It is so easy for Christian leaders to allow other things to become our first love. Almost imperceptibly, the needle of our hearts can move from true north, and before we know it, we have fallen in love with a false idol. Often this surrogate first love seems noble, even Christ-honoring, but it is a heart-killing illusion.

Consider some of the enticements that cry for first place in our hearts:

- Building a successful and growing ministry.
- Being loved by the people we serve and keeping them happy.
- Making a name for ourselves.
- Making enough money to provide for ourselves and those we love.
- Feeling important and valuable in our own hearts.
- Loving and serving the people in our churches or ministries.

The things that can replace God as our first love aren't always bad. They become unhealthy only when they take first place in our hearts. Leaders who plan to serve God faithfully for a lifetime learn to identify when they are tempted to let something else become their first love. We are building healthy lives and ministries when we make sure that God rules supreme and that our hearts are beating passionately for him. When his glory is our joy, when our hearts beat with his, when he rules with no rivals, we grow healthy as leaders.

Network Building
The Power of Prayer

For over a decade, the pastors and interns at Corinth Church have met each Monday morning to seek the face of God in prayer. Before we get revved up for the week, we gather to talk with our Savior. On the first day of the new week, there are always other things to do that seem more urgent, but none is more important. In this time, we have laughed and wept. We have shared joys and burdens. We have bowed our hearts and yielded our wills to the Father. As the years have passed, it has become the rhythm of our souls. If there's a holiday or people are traveling and we miss a Monday-morning prayer time, we feel a sense of loss, because this time has become the core of our week.

This networking time of prayer to kick off each week helps us remember our first priority, our primary passion, the goal of our hearts and ministries. If our hearts are deeply in love with God and he is our first passion, the direction of our week of ministry will be set at true north. On different occasions, I have gathered for this time of prayer with a bad attitude and feeling far from God. But as we have prayed together, my heart has often been recaptured by God and my focus readjusted.

There is something wonderful, life-giving, and perspective-altering about praying with others. As others speak with God, their faith overflows and touches our hearts. The Holy Spirit uses these sacred moments to move in the hearts of those gathered. One Monday morning during our time of prayer, Warren Burgess's prayer inspired me to love Jesus more passionately. I was so moved, I wrote down his words.

He prayed, "O Lord, the longer we walk with you, the more we discover we are children. We need you. We need each other." As Warren prayed, I glanced at him, as I had done so many times before. His hands were open and turned upward, moving gently as one would gesture while talking to a friend. His head was reverently bowed and his eyes were tightly shut, as if fixed on a face far away but so very close.

I saw a little child talking to his daddy. This precious man, almost eighty years old, loves God with a contagious natural ferocity. As we prayed together that day, I grew to love God more.

As leaders, connecting with God more intentionally and intimately is our starting point; it is the foundation for all we do in ministry. When we are falling more deeply in love with God with each passing day, all of our lives are driven by this simple reality: God loves me and I love God.

Loving the People We Are Called to Lead

I admit that I've said it on more than one occasion. I mean it as a joke, but it betrays a painful reality. I'm a little embarrassed to write it, but here it goes: "Ministry would be easy if it weren't for the people!"

In my years of church ministry, I have had my fair share of painful encounters, nasty letters, unfair accusations, and head-butting. I have often thought that there is nothing more satisfying than being a leader in a church, and that there is also nothing more painful. When we open our hearts to those we lead, when we love people, when we sacrifice, when we invest ourselves, we risk getting burned. And I don't know a single Christian leader who has made it far down the road unscathed.

Because I interact regularly with Christian leaders all over the United States and in other parts of the world, I've discovered that some deal with the pain of ministry by shutting off their hearts. They build a wall, an emotional buffer to protect them from being hurt again. They still do the work that is expected of them. They check off all the boxes on their daily to-do lists. They preach sermons, lead youth groups, meet with people, and lock eyes and nod their heads during conversations, but they have safeguarded themselves. They have shut off their hearts.

I understand this, because I have felt tempted to do the same thing. And at different times, I have protected my heart with the armor of cynicism and the moat of emotional distance. When I see myself responding this way, I'm moved to increase my efforts to love the people I am called to serve. I ask God to help me have the courage to love people even when it could mean personal pain. I invite the Holy Spirit to bring to mind the wonderful moments I've experienced in my years of church ministry. I fix my eyes on Jesus and remember how he served, loved, and sacrificed himself for the very people whose sin put him on the cross.

Network Building
Make Space to Bless

At Corinth Church, it's a tradition that the core staff treats each member of the staff to lunch on their birthday. During that lunch, each person around the table shares words of blessing for that person. The staff members reflect on the past year and express appreciation for how God has used this person, how they have grown, or a way they have touched lives. When we first began this practice, some of the staff members were very uncomfortable being the center of attention. In particular, Barb Velhdeer and Debi Rose would squirm, blush, and struggle to sit there and take such lavish affirmation. But this has become a deeply appreciated time that each staff person looks forward to and enjoys.

We need to remember that right on the heels of Jesus' call to love God with all that is in us, he said, "This is the first and greatest commandment. And the second is like it: 'Love your neighbor as yourself.' All the Law and the Prophets hang on these two commandments" (Matt. 22:38–40). Jesus understood that an authentic relationship with God leads to a deep love for people. These two commandments are inseparable. Yet if we are not careful, we can forget this call to a deep love for the people we lead. When we forget Jesus' words and just seek to do the work of ministry, we can disregard the fact that people matter to God.

The movie *Braveheart* portrays two dramatically contrasting visions of leadership. On the one hand is William Wallace, the leader of the Scottish army. Although there are nobles in the land, they are more concerned with their position, lands, and wealth than with the people. But Wallace has inspired the people, and they follow him into battle again and again. The operative word is follow. Wallace is always the first onto the field. He loves the people and their nation. He fights at their side and bleeds with them.

After one epic battle during which the Scottish forces route the invading English army, the nobles decide it would be expedient to knight Wallace and then co-opt him. They all have ties to Edward the Longshanks, the king of England. They don't have a vision of a free Scotland but are more concerned with covering their political butts.

After they knight Wallace, they begin to quibble over ancestral rights and try to pull Wallace into their ongoing internal battles. He refuses to play along. As the mood in the room deteriorates, he and his group of core leaders begin to walk out. The nobles ask him where he is going, and the following dialogue unfolds:

William Wallace	We have beaten the English, but they'll come back because you won't stand together.
Nobles	What will you do?
Wallace	I'll invade England and defeat the English on their own ground.
Nobles	Invade, that's impossible.
Wallace	Why? Why is that impossible? You're so concerned with squabbling for the scraps from Longshanks' table that you've missed

your God-given right for something better. There's a difference between us. You think the people of this country exist to provide you with position. I think your position exists to provide those people with freedom, and I go to make sure they have it!

Wallace's words uncover a sinister motive in the nobles' hearts. They see the people as stepping stones to their place of position. They do not love the people. Wallace reminds them that maybe, just maybe, they have been put in their place of leadership so that they can give to the people. Maybe their place of authority and influence should compel them to serve those they lead.

Yet another example of leadership occurs later in the movie. Longshanks, the king of England, is in command of his forces. He does not ride into battle, take up a sword, or risk getting even a scratch on his body. Instead, he stays out of the fray, at a safe distance, and gives orders.

The battle takes its twists and turns until the English have the upper hand. From his place of safety, Longshanks looks at the battlefield. The English soldiers clearly are defeating the Scottish and Irish forces. Then, Longshanks says one word: "Archers!" He calls for his commander to summon the archers to send volleys of arrows into the battlefield.

His captain says, "Beg pardon. Sire, won't we hit our own troops?"

Longshanks responds, "Yes, but we'll hit theirs as well," and as an afterthought, he mutters, "We have reserves." Longshanks says the word again, "Archers!" The flag is raised and the captain waves his arm. Volleys of arrows fly, hitting Irish, Scottish, and English troops.

As the scene ends, Longshanks turns to ride off and says, "Send us news of our victory. Shall we retire?"

Throughout the interchange, Longshanks is dispassionate. He clearly doesn't care about the people he has "led" into battle. They are pawns on his military chessboard. They are dispensable. Longshanks does not love these people.

As leaders, we must be sure we never grow to see the people we lead as cogs in a machine or pawns on a chessboard. We can't let our hearts grow cold or distant. If we're going to lead like Jesus, we must allow the dangerous power of love to fill our hearts. We can't become like the nobles in *Braveheart*, who see the people as a means to maintaining their own position or even elevating themselves.

In recent years, I have observed something I have never seen in the church before. I call it the Rock Star Syndrome. There is a new generation of church leaders who are treated like rock stars. They are elevated. They are exalted. They are the stars of the show. When people come to church and the Rock Star is not present, the "audience" feels cheated. One senses that if this leader were to leave that church, many of the attendees would leave also. The crowds are not there to engage in the life of the body of Christ. They aren't there to discover their gifts and faithfully serve. They have come to taste the flavor of the month.

I worry as this phenomenon spreads, because these leaders seem to like and even encourage their "untouchable" status. They build a moat between themselves and the people in the church. Often even their staff can't get to them for a conversation or for prayer. They are unapproachable.

Self-Examination Suggestion
What Kind of Leader?

Am I a leader like Wallace, like the nobles, or like Longshanks? Take some time to reflect on this question. Honestly look at your leadership life, your motives, and how you relate (or don't relate) to people.

A leader like Wallace. Am I first onto the battlefield? Do I labor and fight side-by-side with the people I lead? Are people devoted to me because they know I love them and would lay my life down for them?

continued ⇨

A leader like the nobles. Do I see the people I lead as means to help me maintain my position? Do I treat people like stepping stones to advance myself? Do I sense that the people I lead don't really trust me because they can see that I care more about myself than about them?

A leader like Longshanks. Do I stand back, out of the fray, and let the people I lead do all the hard work? Do I see people as dispensable, as pawns on my ministry chessboard? Have I allowed my heart to become so hard that I don't care when the people I lead are hurting, weary, or broken?

Being a Christian leader is dangerous business. It means opening our hearts, loving people, sacrificing, and risking great pain. But there is no other way to be a leader. This is the way of Jesus. He loved the people he led so much that he laid down his life. We too must lead with this kind of love.

A Forgiving Heart

"Then Peter came to Jesus and asked, 'Lord, how many times shall I forgive my brother when he sins against me? Up to seven times?' Jesus answered, 'I tell you, not seven times, but seventy-seven times'" (Matt. 18:21–22). Christian leaders are called to love God and those they lead. There is no better laboratory for learning to love than ministry. There is also no better place to learn the art of forgiveness than in the life of the church. The church is filled with people. People are broken and sinful. Spend enough time in the church and you will be hurt. And when you are nursing the wounds and still feeling the sharp pain inflicted by a brother or sister, you will hear Jesus' voice calling you to forgive.

When Jesus was reviled, he did not retaliate. When he was mocked, he prayed for forgiveness. When the Savior was denied three times by Peter, he rose from the dead and called Peter back to himself and to a place of fruitful ministry. No one spends much time in ministry serving God and his people without getting burned. When we hit these emotional and spiritual crossroads, we have to decide whether we will walk the way of forgiveness or allow our hearts to grow cold and take a "never again" posture.

Because pain and heartache are part of ministry, it's possible for every single Christian leader to become angry, hurt, cynical, and insulated. If we don't learn the wisdom and power of forgiveness, our hearts will die and we will become shells of the leaders God wants us to be. I learned this lesson early in my ministry.

One of my most painful leadership lessons came shortly after I graduated from seminary and began to work in a church as a full-time pastor and leader. I was asked to be on a committee that worked with incoming seminary students who were training for full-time ministry. One of our responsibilities was to determine if students had financial needs.

At my first meeting, this group looked over four requests for financial aid from a special denominational fund. Years earlier, a church had closed and had put all of its assets in this special fund, which was to be used to help train future pastors and leaders for the denomination. Each request was handled quickly and efficiently; any student with need who planned to go into ministry in our denomination would receive two thousand dollars a year. Because my wife and I had struggled financially through our years of seminary, it was a joy to approve giving money to these seminary students.

After we had made the approvals, I commented to the chair of the committee that I wished this fund had been around the past three years because both my wife and I would have qualified for these grants and could have borrowed $10,000 less in student loans.

I had assumed this fund had just come into existence. Each of the years I was in seminary, I had asked my pastor if there were any sources of support for struggling seminary students. Each time I asked for his help, I got a speech about how hard things were back when he went through school. He told me that I should "learn to eat cold beans out of a can." (I'm still not sure how my character would grow if I kept the beans in the can and refused to heat them.) He had assured me, on many occasions, that there was no support available (from the church or the denomination) and told me I needed to suck it up, toughen up, and eat lots of beans … cold, if possible.

As I sat with the committee members, I was stunned to hear the chair say, "This fund has been in place for over a decade." I was dumbfounded. You see, the place that I had filled on the committee was previously occupied by none other than my pastor for the past three years. In a private conversation, I asked the chair if there was any way this person hadn't known about these funds being available for me and my wife, and confided that we had struggled profoundly while in seminary. (We had lived well under the poverty level all three years.) He assured me that my friend and partner in ministry had voted to offer this money to many other students over the past three years.

I was saddened.

I was angry.

I felt sick to my stomach.

The chair of the committee tried to console me and actually investigated the possibility of giving us this support retroactively as payment toward our student loans. But the decision was that doing so would set a bad precedent. I swallowed hard and decided to consider it a lesson learned.

Out of this, I committed to do all I could to help seminary students get through school with minimal debt. I also learned to forgive someone who had wronged me. I had to decide whether I would feed my bitterness or find a way to forgive. It was a battle. I honestly considered not forgiving him. But by God's grace, and in the shadow of the cross, I chose to forgive.

We worked together for a number of years and experienced a fruitful ministry. If I had not chosen to forgive him, I would have been filled with resentment and anger. Instead, I allowed myself to wonder why he felt the need to see us struggle. I didn't agree with the way he handled me, but I did forgive him. I decided to treat him as if he had never wronged me. I also recognized that this unkindness wasn't characteristic of how he treated me. In general, he was very supportive and loving. Though I will never understand why he hid potential support from me, I was able to serve side-by-side with this brother and find joy in our partnership.

If our hearts are going to be healthy and strong, we will learn to forgive. There's no question that we will have many opportunities to do so. The choice is ours.

I've Got Your Back
Help Me Forgive

Forgiveness heals. Unforgiveness kills. Meet separately with two people in your ministry who love you and whom you trust. Ask the following questions, inviting them to be honest with you:

- Is there anyone who has wronged me whom you feel I have not fully forgiven?
- What would you recommend I do to restore this relationship and forgive this person?
- Do you know of anyone I have wronged whose forgiveness I need to ask?

Listen closely to these two people, pray about their input, and seek reconciliation.

A Heart for the Lost

Compassion. It marked Jesus' life. Look into the Savior's heart: "Jesus went through all the towns and villages, teaching in their synagogues, preaching the good news of the kingdom and healing every disease and sickness. When he saw the crowds, he had compassion on them, because they were harassed and helpless, like sheep without a shepherd" (Matt. 9:35–36). This is a prelude to Jesus' statement that "the harvest is plentiful but the workers are few" and to his call for us to "ask the Lord of the harvest, therefore, to send out workers into his harvest fields" (vv. 37–38). Jesus' heart broke for those who hadn't yet received his amazing grace and experienced the Father's love.

As Christian leaders, we are to reflect our Savior's heart. This means we are to allow our hearts to be broken over those who are lost. Our hearts should be so affected that we are compelled to pray and to enter the harvest fields. One indicator that our hearts are beating strong is when we are moved by compassion and reach out to those who are not yet part of God's family.

Too many leaders have become so busy at their churches or in their ministries that they have no time to connect with those who don't know Jesus. We can become isolated to the point that we almost never relate with people who are lost. We need to hear Jesus' call to pray for harvest workers. And we need to offer ourselves to this Great Commission work.

Self-Examination Suggestion

Making Space

Print a copy of your work and personal schedules for the last week and for the coming week. Get two highlighters of different colors. With one highlighter, mark all the time in the past week that you spent doing church work or connecting primarily with people who already know Jesus. Then with the other highlighter mark the time you spent primarily with those who are outside of God's family. Evaluate whether you are intentionally spending significant time with people who do not yet have a relationship with Jesus.

Next look at the coming week. Mark the times you plan to do church work and be with believers. With the other highlighter, mark the times you have blocked out to go into the harvest fields and connect with those who are spiritually disconnected. If the exercise shows that you need to spend more time with those who are not yet in God's family, make changes in your schedule. If you find this exercise helpful, do it again next week and make it a regular part of your planning.

At Corinth Church, we have made it a point to check in regularly and ask each other about the people in our lives whom we are seeking to reach. In staff meetings, we often make time to share about the people in our lives who are spiritually disconnected. Each time we share about these people, three things happen:

1. We permit and encourage staff members to make time in their lives and space in their hearts for lost people.
2. We invite the whole group to pray for each other in the area of personal evangelism.
3. We create a sense of corporate accountability in our personal outreach.

Jesus was filled with compassion for those who were lost and wandering like sheep without a shepherd. His heart broke for them. If we are to have the heart of Jesus, we must make time to connect with those who are far from God. As we spend time in close relationship with lost people, as we grow to love them, we will be moved to share the amazing grace we have experienced.

Network Building
Strategic Shopping

If you find that your schedule is jam-packed and you just don't have time to connect with people outside of your ministry, one way to begin is by becoming a strategic shopper. Make it a point to buy gas, groceries, and even meals at the same place. As you do, slow down! Look at the people who work behind the counter or serve you at your table. Pray for them. Ask God to give you a heart for these people. Look at their name badges or ask them their names. Build relationships that might become redemptive with time. You'll be amazed at how quickly you begin to care for others and how freely they will share their lives and needs with you.

Over the years, the staff at Corinth Church has dined frequently at a number of restaurants near our church. As we built relationships with many of the owners and workers in these places, beautiful things happened. One of the restaurants decided to begin serving a lunch and dinner buffet, and they made little handwritten placards for each item on the menu. In a short time, these became quite ragged. So our office team took a menu, made a very sharp placard for each item, and laminated it. Then we put all of them in a little box in alphabetical order. When we gave this small gift to the owners, they were overwhelmed. They offered to pay us, but we let them know that we love them and just wanted to serve them and their business.

When we dine out, we often have the opportunity to pray for our server or some other employee. Once we have established a friendship, it's natural to ask if there's anything we can pray about for them. They know we are "church workers," and they expect this kind of thing. When it feels right, someone from our staff will say, "Before we have our meal, we say a short prayer. If you have a need you'd feel comfortable sharing with us, we'd love to pray for you." In almost every case, the person shares freely, and often surprisingly deeply. In most cases, they head back to work after sharing, and we pray for them and our meal. But we have also had servers share a need and then stand right at the table as we pray. A few have even grabbed the hand of a staff member as we lifted up their need. Over the years, some of the needs we have prayed for are sick children, strength to quit smoking, broken marriages, help in reconnecting with God, and even for a new job (which we prayed for very quietly).

In our discussion of the anatomy of a leader, we could have started with a number of different body parts, but the heart always comes first. When our hearts beat strong, the rest of our bodies can draw life from them. When our hearts are weak, it's difficult to be healthy in any other area of leadership. When our hearts are passionate about God, tender toward those we lead, willing to forgive, and compassionate toward the lost, we are on the path to healthy leadership.

chapter 2

Lifelong Learning Expands Our Horizons

The Leader's Mind

My life is busy... too busy. Most weeks I have more items on my to-do list than I can accomplish. I push things back to next week, I toss out things that aren't urgent, and I run around like a triage nurse putting bandages on the worst wounds so that no one bleeds out on my shift. The luxury of reading a book, digging into some new topic of study, or sitting quietly and reflecting on God's Word for personal edification is often squeezed out by the pressing needs I face each day. Yet in the quiet of the night, when I put my reeling mind to bed, I wish for more. In all of my doing and serving and ministering, I sincerely long to think deeply about the things of God, to sit at the feet of Jesus, to exercise this increasingly flabby mind of mine so that it will be an instrument worthy of the God I serve.

> Finally, brothers, whatever is true, whatever is noble, whatever is right, whatever is pure, whatever is lovely, whatever is admirable—if anything is excellent or praiseworthy—think about such things.
>
> —Philippians 4:8

> Oh, how I love your law! I meditate on it all day long. Your commands make me wiser than my enemies, for they are ever with me.
>
> —Psalm 119:97–98

I can't remember ever seeing a Bible as I grew up. My family didn't go to church, and the concept of reading the "Holy Scriptures" wasn't on our radar. When I became a follower of Jesus in my adolescent years, I was a blank slate. I had learned the basic gospel story by listening to the youth pastor at the church I had started to attend, but that was it. I had no idea Christmas or Easter had any religious significance. The only biblical text I had heard or could recognize was the narrative of Jesus' birth as quoted by Linus in the Charlie Brown Christmas show that came on TV each holiday season. I still remember the first time I read the gospel of Luke and realized that when Linus was explaining the true meaning of Christmas to Charlie Brown, he was quoting the Bible. I was shocked.

Symptoms Check

My Mind Is Flabby

- [ ] I find myself recycling messages and illustrations because I have nothing new to say.
- [ ] When I finish my must-do list each day, I am so frazzled that all I can do is sit in front of the TV and zone out.

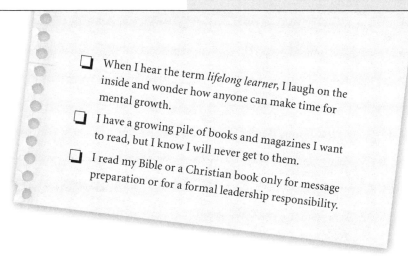

☐ When I hear the term *lifelong learner*, I laugh on the inside and wonder how anyone can make time for mental growth.

☐ I have a growing pile of books and magazines I want to read, but I know I will never get to them.

☐ I read my Bible or a Christian book only for message preparation or for a formal leadership responsibility.

The week I became a Christian, the life of my mind changed ... dramatically. I received my first instruction in spiritual growth. I was given a Bible. It was a hardback, RSV Harper Study Bible. As far as I can recollect, I had never held a Bible in my hands before. I had certainly never been given my own Bible or encouraged to read this ancient text. I was just a fifteen-year-old kid who had come to faith in Jesus, and one of the volunteer college-aged leaders decided I needed a Bible.

Here is a synopsis of my training. He gave me my fresh new Bible and said, "Now that you are a Christian, you are supposed to read this every day." I assured him I would and I got started. In about three months, I went to the young man who had given me the Bible and asked him what I should read next. He asked me how far I had gotten in my Bible, and I told him, "I'm all done."

I was ready for my next assignment. He looked a little surprised, paused thoughtfully, and said, "Read it again!"

I know that those who have in-depth training in discipleship theory would find this rudimentary form of instruction questionable, but I think it was actually good for me. I did what he said. I read the Bible again and have kept doing so ever since. Each year, I try to read a different translation or paraphrase. I have loved the vivid narrative, struggled with complex theological issues, been challenged by piercing and convicting truth, been confused by historical and contextual issues, been shocked by the gore and bloodshed, been transported into the presence of Jesus, and been transformed by this mysterious Word of God.

The Place of God's Word

Almost thirty years later, I have more questions than when I first became a follower of Jesus. But I also have more answers than I ever dreamed of. I can honestly say I'm beginning to understand the heart of the psalmist when he wrote:

> Oh, how I love your law!
>   I meditate on it all day long....
> How sweet are your words to my taste,
>   sweeter than honey to my mouth!
> I gain understanding from your precepts;
>   therefore I hate every wrong path.
> Your word is a lamp to my feet
>   and a light for my path.
>
> —Psalm 119:97, 103–5

The Bible is the most mind-expanding book in human history. Because it is breathed from the very lungs of God (2 Tim. 3:16), it brings life, hope, power, and direction to those who read it. This book has shaped the minds of leaders for thousands of years. Those who read it and listen for the still small voice of God's Spirit will find the wisdom they need for the countless challenging situations they face in their leadership role.

Priorities Matter

It might seem strange to read an exhortation for Christian leaders to commit to reading the Bible. But I have been reminded far too many times how easy it is to neglect this discipline. I discovered this as a young pastor when I was asked to be on a team that mentored and supported emerging leaders. A group of eight seminary students were being trained in local congregations during their studies. I began meeting with this energetic and passionate group

Network Building
Making God's Word a Priority

Our core staff at Corinth Church meets every Wednesday to plan, pray, connect, and make sure we are tracking together in ministry. One of the things we've done over the years is keep each other accountable to grow spiritually. In particular, we have made it a priority to help each other be faithful in reading the Bible. As the years have passed, we have done this in a variety of ways. Here are some examples:

- Each person shares what they have been reading in God's Word over the past week and shares one way God has spoken to them in their personal Bible study.
- Each person keeps a daily record of their Bible reading and gives it to a pastor every week.
- Each person keeps a journal of their reading and learning, and for accountability shares how they are doing with one other staff member.
- We follow a reading plan (one year we walked through the Old Testament) and share what we are learning.

These are just a few examples. The format has changed over the years, but we've always made it a priority to make sure all of the key church leaders are immersed in the Word of God.

to create a support network for them as they went through their formal training.

Early on, we were sitting in a restaurant having a time of informal interaction when I casually asked the group to share what they were learning as they studied God's Word. A few of them began to talk about what they were learning in class and in their preparation for preaching or teaching a Sunday school class. I jumped in and clarified, "What I meant to ask is, what are you learning as you read God's Word for your own spiritual growth?"

The table became very quiet and I received eight blank stares.

We had a fascinating conversation about the difference between studying the Bible for personal spiritual growth and for teaching others. We concluded that we read the Bible differently as we are preparing to teach, preach, or instruct. We agreed that reading the Bible for the sole purpose of soul development feels different and yields another kind of fruit. Both types of reading are needed in a leader's life. Unfortunately, we are often measured by the fruit of our formal study, and no one seems to notice whether we read the Bible for personal growth.

In our conversation, a very interesting statement caught my attention. One young man said, "I have always had personal devotions and read the Bible for my own spiritual growth. I believe it is very important. But I am in seminary and also working in a church. I am too busy right now. When I get out of seminary and am working in the church, when my schedule finally slows down, I will reestablish a habit of reading the Bible for personal growth." I asked the others in the group if they were in a similar place. To a person, they admitted they had put personal Bible study on the shelf while in seminary. Each one planned to reload this discipline after their formal training.

They were shocked when I told them, "This is the most free time you will ever have. When you begin your ministry, you will be busier than you are now." We talked about why it's important to make personal Bible study part of our daily rhythm in all the seasons of life. And the group committed to pray for each other and to keep each other accountable to read the Bible regularly for their own edification, both while they were in seminary and long afterward.

Christian leaders, particularly those in church ministry, are often tempted to substitute their lesson preparation for personal time feeding on the rich banquet of God's Word. This is problematic because our minds and hearts tune in differently when we are getting ready to teach others. Our "audience" is in the front of our mind, as it should be. There is no question that leaders learn a great deal at these times, but we gain different kinds of insights. As valuable as this learning is, it's not a surrogate for time set aside to meet with God face-to-face and ask what the Spirit wants to say to us.

Help from My Friends
How Do You Nurture Your Soul and Connection to God?

On a daily basis, I need to be closely connected with God, through time with him in prayer and in his Word. For years, I have used the vintage Robert Murray McCheyne Daily Bible Calendar to help guide my devotional reading. Before I read, I will simply ask, "God, would you reveal yourself to me as I read?" Then I read interactively with him and connect with God through conversational prayer.

— Nancy Grisham, PhD, Evangelism Leader, Livin' Ignited

Leaders who want to experience a continual process of mind expansion are wise to make time in their daily schedules to pull away from all distractions and sit at Jesus' feet. For some, a quiet time of solitude first thing in the morning is perfect. For others, the middle of the day or the evening works best. Whatever time of day you designate, make sure it's prime time when the mind is fresh and distractions are few. Leaders who regularly meet with God, open the Word, and listen in receptive prayer will find their minds expanded with rich truth and prepared for the challenges that lie ahead.

Allowing Others Leverage in Your Life

Since it's often a challenge to make time for these holy meetings with God, it's helpful to build in lines of accountability. At Corinth Church, we have leveraged the built-in network of the church board. Rather than starting our monthly meetings with a perfunctory prayer and diving into business, we devote the first hour of our evening to small group prayer and reflecting on the Word. In our church tradition, the board is made up of the elders, deacons, and pastors. Each month, these leaders spend time in groups of five or six to discuss a series of questions for mutual learning and accountability:

1. *How many days a week have you spent time reading God's Word and seeking the face of God in prayer?* Each leader is given a sheet to keep a record of their personal time in God's Word.
2. *What is one lesson you learned from your personal Bible study this month?* This gives each leader a chance to teach the other small group members. It also affords the other group members an opportunity to receive insight from four or five other leaders they respect.
3. *How have you sought to serve and love a member of your family in the past month?* We desire to help our leaders make family a priority, and this question creates an opportunity for support in this arena of life.
4. *How can we pray for you?* This leads to a time of mutual prayer for personal, family, ministry, and work needs.

Our church board has grown to love this monthly time of accountability, support, and mutual learning. A number of them have said that knowing they are going to give a report on their time in personal Bible study has spurred them to higher levels of commitment. They have also made it clear that their spiritual lives and effectiveness as leaders have grown with their expanding knowledge of God's Word. Some have reported that hearing others share about their journeys of learning from the Bible has challenged them to dig deeper into this glorious book.

One of the things we learned in the development of leaders in our church is that a commitment to be a student of God's Word is essential for maximum effectiveness. As our leaders grow in their knowledge of the Word, their leadership potential explodes. Another by-product of this commitment is a higher level of unity in our meetings. We have always had a strong sense of common mission, but as our leaders feed on the truth of Scripture and lift each other up in their spiritual disciplines, we reach new levels of visionary focus. Meetings that might otherwise feel laborious and tense are joyous and peace-filled. And for some reason, though we take about an hour to share and pray, our meetings don't take as long as they used to.

Help from My Friends

How Do You Nurture Your Soul and Connection to God?

Ten years ago, a friend called me, and during our conversation, he complained that he didn't feel closely connected with God. I bluntly said, "And whose fault is that?" Then I said, "Okay, by next Friday, let's both read the first six chapters of Matthew." I called him a week later, and he was very excited. His connection with God was growing stronger. I said, "Let's read the next six chapters of Matthew, and I'll call next Friday." Thirteen years later, we have read through the Bible three times, and we are starting a fourth time through. Both of us are closely connected to God. And as a huge bonus, our four-year Bible reading program has spread. Now over two thousand people at Faith Church have joined us. The connection to God is amazing. The emails, conversations, and notes of life-change are incredible. Way to go, God!

— Bob Bouwer, Senior Pastor, Faith Church, Dyer, IN

A Natural Partnership

Wise leaders know how to leverage every relationship as a tool for spiritual growth. My wife and I have discovered tremendous value in helping each other grow in the love and knowledge of God's Word. Early in our marriage, we tried to sit down to study the Bible together. Honestly, it didn't work out very well. Most of the time we would end up analyzing the text, and the experience felt more academic than devotional. Both Sherry and I are fairly strong personalities, we are both passionate leaders, and we both have seminary degrees. I know that many couples share rich times in devotional study, but this was not our experience. But we were convinced that spiritual growth as a couple was important, so we kept working at it.

With time, we discovered how to best inspire each other to grow in love with God's Word. Each evening, we spend time debriefing, sharing about our day. One of the things we seek to do is share what we learned in our personal Bible study. I can't count how many insights and life-transforming lessons I have learned from listening to Sherry tell about what God is teaching her as she studies the Bible. I am also confident that God uses the insights I share to shape her life. Each of us has found that this rhythm of informal reporting and reflecting has contributed to our spiritual growth curve.

Committed to Lifelong Learning

I've stopped asking the question.

I use to ask it all the time when I met another leader. I wanted to learn from them, so I would pick their brain with a whole series of questions. But I've dropped this particular one from my list of queries.

Unless I know the person well and am sure they have an answer, I spare them the embarrassment. I stopped asking the question because I received too many blank stares, saw too many awkward glances at the ground, and heard too many uncomfortable explanations about how "things have been really busy lately."

The question is, "What have you been reading lately?"

I used to find that many leaders were always engaged with a book or two. I learned a great deal from the subsequent conversations we had about what they were learning from their reading, and I would often go out and get a copy of a book at their recommendation.

I remember meeting a fascinating leader from a Mennonite background as I was flying home from the West Coast. He raved about Gene Edwards' books *A Tale of Three Kings* and *The Prisoner in the Third Cell*. As I later read these beautifully written stories about King David and John the Baptist, they touched my heart and spoke to me about the sovereignty of God, a leader's need for humility, and the importance of trusting Jesus no matter what we face. After reading these two books, I mined the rest of Edwards' body of work and found a number of other helpful books, including *How to Prevent a Church Split*. This straightforward, gut-wrenching reflection on the spiritual cost of bloody church splits has had a huge impact on how I deal with conflict and tension in the church. I am so thankful I crossed paths with a leader who was committed to being a lifelong learner.

It's important that we exercise our minds. I suppose I'm preaching to the choir. You are reading a book right now! I want to bless you, affirm that you are a rare breed, and encourage you to continue this commitment to be a learner. Digging into books is one of the best ways to keep growing as a leader. There is a wealth of learning at our fingertips if we simply pick up a worthwhile book and read it. The challenge is finding helpful books in a day when there seems to be more published than ever before. How do we find theological texts that are worth our time, classic books on the spiritual disciplines that will speak to our hungry hearts, leadership books from Christian and secular authors that are must-reads, commentaries that are insightful and helpful, novels that will spark our imagination and stretch our thinking, and other books that will expand our minds?

A wise leader must discover where to mine for intellectual gold in the growing mountain of books. We can't read everything, so we have to identify the best places to dig. One excellent way to discover helpful books is by developing a network of fellow leaders who are passionate readers. Allowing colleagues and friends to give you wise direction can save time and money. Not every book recommended to you will hit the mark, but many will.

Network Building
Creating a Resource Team

It is an informal alliance at best, but I have a network of people who help me expand my mind through their consistent suggestion of "you gotta read this one" books. My team crosses generations, gender, and continents. Wise leaders will build an eclectic group of fellow learners who cheer them on. Here are some key players who have been on my team:

Person	Ministry and Personal Background	Areas in Which This Person Influences Me
Dr. Charles Van Engen	Teaches theology of world missions at Fuller Seminary	Missions, theology, and worldview
Sherry Harney	Author, speaker, and my wife	Spiritual formation and prayer
Todd Van Ek	Church pastor and member of a pastors small group with me	Leadership and church administration
Lammert Vrieling	Church-planting leader in Geneva, Switzerland	Emerging cultural trends, business, and social change
Lee Strobel and Mark Mittelberg	Authors and partners in developing evangelism strategies	Evangelism, apologetics, and social change
Adam Barr	Former intern at Corinth, now leader of Borderlands Ministries	Worldview issues and general reading
Ryan Pazdur	Former intern and current staff member at Corinth Church	Commentaries

All of these people influence me as they share what they are learning in their studies and as they give me recommendations for reading. One of these team members, Todd Van Ek, will often highlight the most insightful sections of a book he has read, then type them up and share them with friends. I have surveyed a number of books by reading Todd's notes. Lammert Vrieling recommended I read *The Tipping Point* by Malcom Gladwell. This book became one of the influential forces in my writing the book *Seismic Shifts*. The influence of this group on the shaping of my mind is hard to calculate.

Since many leaders are not committed readers, it's essential that those who want to be lifelong learners identify others who are passionate about nurturing the world of the mind. When you find friends like this, even if they live thousands of miles away, maintain those relationships. They are precious gifts.

Mental Exercises

Reading isn't the only way to grow as a lifelong learner. I'm focusing on it because it seems to be a dwindling discipline. Here are a few other suggestions:

Conferences and seminars. We live in a day in which there are more conferences available for us to attend than at any time in history. There are gatherings on virtually every topic imaginable. Although they take time and money to attend, these kinds of experiences, if you pick the right ones, are great investments. Not only do you learn from them but you have the opportunity to network with other like-minded leaders and usually leave with a pile of ideas, resources, and books for further study.

Magazines, newspapers, internet portals, and blogs. Supplement your diet of books with other forms of literature. A local or national paper and the cover page of most internet search engines put a leader in touch with hot topics in politics, culture, fashion, sports, and everything else that's on the minds of those you serve. Subscribing to a handful of magazines can help you keep your thumb on the pulse of thoughts and trends in the church and society. And wandering through select blogs can open windows onto the human condition.

Movies and TV shows. Some Christian leaders have turned off their TVs and boycotted movies altogether. This might be helpful for some people, but leaders who want their minds tuned in to the currents of culture are wise to selectively view what's hot on TV and in the movies. I'm not advocating voyeurism disguised as cultural research, however. A vast wasteland of garbage is being produced, and leaders need to guard their minds against the lure of inappropriate viewing. But leaders who want to interact in a meaningful way with their world need to be familiar with media trends.

Continuing education classes. Most leaders live close enough to a college or seminary to audit an occasional class. In many cases, the cost is nominal. Attending classes provides opportunities to build relationships, grapple with new ideas, and reinforce past learning. If you don't live near an institution of higher education, you can take advantage of a growing number of options for online continuing education.

Colloquy groups. Some leaders learn well through informal discussion and verbal bantering. This interactive form of learning is often required in college, seminary, or other formal educational settings but is rarely practiced after someone is "out of school." Colloquy groups are small gatherings of people who agree to gather, study, and dig into a topic for a set period of time. The key learning element in a setting like this is group interaction.

Too many leaders shift their minds into neutral after they begin their full-time professional lives. Because they are busy, sick of school, or just don't want to hassle with it, their commitment to expanding the mind is anemic at best. Some believe that when they finish their formal education, they have nailed down all the learning needed for a lifetime. Unfortunately, they are missing out on the personal growth, benefits to the church, and joy of being a lifelong learner.

I even suggest that leaders read books written by authors who challenge their worldview and rattle their cage. I find that reading books by someone who stands on the other side of the fence from me can be very enlightening.

A leader with an expanding mind commits to be a student, a learner, a continuous explorer of the landscape of new ideas and fresh ways to approach old issues, truths, and challenges. Being a lifelong learner is a decision. It's an attitude that says there are still intellectual mountains to climb, mental exercises to perform, and countless lessons to be learned.

I've Got Your Back
Sharing Great Resources

Every leader can name certain books that have influenced them. As I think about supporting and walking with other leaders, a number of books rise to the top of my recommendation list. I keep extra copies of them so I'll always have one to give away, which is a natural way for me to support and help other leaders whom I care about. My list of books covers many topics and areas of life:

continued ⟳

Who I Recommend This Book To	Title and Author	Description
Those facing a time of deep loss and pain	A Grace Disguised, Jerry Sittser	Jerry Sittser tells the story of watching three generations of the women in his family (his wife, mother, and four-year-old daughter) die on the side of the road after a drunk driver struck his car. The book focuses not only on his story but also on what each of us faces in our times of loss. It also gives hope of God's surprising grace in the darkest times.
Those who are overextended, stressed, and out of balance	Making Room for Life, Randy Frazee	In this practical and challenging book, Randy Frazee tells his story of spinning out of balance and how God can help us restore a healthy life rhythm.
Business leaders who are successful but unfulfilled	Halftime, Bob Buford	Bob Buford shares his story of changing his life plan from success to significance and helps others begin this same journey.
Those in a time of spiritual dryness	The Prayer Devotional Bible, Ben Patterson	The Scripture readings and daily devotions in this book are powerful and refresh the soul and stretch the mind.
People who want to hone their leadership gift	Courageous Leadership, Bill Hybels	This is an excellent book not only for veterans but also for people just entering the leadership arena. Bill Hybels tackles all the big issues ministry leaders face.
Leaders who are feeling discouraged	Jesus Driven Ministry, Ajith Fernando	Ajith serves in Sri Lanka, one of the most difficult places to be a Christian leader in our day and age. He understands the theology of suffering better than any person I have encountered, and his writings will strengthen and encourage weary leaders.
Those who need a good laugh and a humorous look at the challenges of leading in the church	The Philippian Fragment, Calvin Miller	What leaders who are feeling spent often need is a good laugh. This classic book is the perfect prescription.
Leaders who are dealing with blurred relational boundaries	Lambs on the Ledge, Joyce Strong	The chapter on emotional adultery can be a life-saving resource for leaders who have become emotionally involved with a person to whom or with whom they minister.

These are just a few of the titles I find myself recommending frequently. I suggest that you keep your own list of books you can share with other leaders and even keep a couple of extra copies of these books around to give away when the opportunity arises. One way we can watch each other's backs is by pointing each other to the resources we need to remain healthy, faithful, and effective in ministry.

God has given each of us a mind to use for his glory and purposes. To the casual observer, most leaders appear to be diligent about mind development, an understandable assumption. But busy schedules, the stress of leadership, and even laziness get in the way of intellectual growth. Wise leaders take time to evaluate the condition of their mind. Is it being sharpened to a razor's edge or becoming a bowl of mush?

Self-Examination Suggestion
Mind Exam

Reflect on the following questions on your own, with a mentor, or in a small group of trusted friends. Pray for humility and honesty as you examine the world of your mind.

1. How much time do I devote to learning from books written by great thinkers and practitioners?
2. What book have I read recently that was written from a perspective radically different from mine? What did I learn from this book?

continued ⟳

3. Who do I respect who is an avid reader? Am I willing to ask this person for recommended reading?

4. What am I doing to saturate my mind with Scripture?

5. When is my prime time of the day for mental acuity? What can I do to carve out some of this time to read and meditate on God's Word?

chapter 3

Attentive Listening Informs Wise Decisions

The Leader's Ears

I listen. It's what I do. When couples come to me with struggles and problems, I listen. When neighbors face a loss or relational meltdown, they come to me. I listen. When other leaders whom I respect offer wisdom and insight, I engage, interact, and listen. When staff members or leaders in my ministry are processing the challenges of leading in the church, I listen. When the still small voice of the Holy Spirit calls my name, I tune in, I quiet my heart, Spirit calls my name, I tune in, I quiet my heart, I slow down, I listen. Lord, in this very noisy world, teach me to listen with even greater intensity. Help me to recognize your voice speaking to me in so many different ways.

> I tell you the truth, the man who does not enter the sheep pen by the gate, but climbs in by some other way, is a thief and a robber. The man who enters by the gate is the shepherd of his sheep. The watchman opens the gate for him, and the sheep listen to his voice. He calls his own sheep by name and leads them out. When he has brought out all his own, he goes on ahead of them, and his sheep follow him because they know his voice.
>
> —John 10:1–4

> Be still, and know that I am God.
>
> —Psalm 46:10

I'm sitting in an airport terminal writing while waiting to get on a plane to Chicago. A man sits just behind my left shoulder, talking on his cell phone about airflow technology and why his company offers the best equipment on the market. A young woman three seats to my left is knitting with green yarn, chatting on her cell phone with her boyfriend about how much she misses him already, though he just dropped her off at the airport. (They seem to be quite in love.) Both of these conversations are much louder than they need to be. As I try to write about listening to God's voice, they chatter on and the intercom kicks in, adding to the chorus of distractions. An announcement blares that a flight bound for Chicago is about to finish boarding and take off. I stop typing because I hear "Chicago" and wonder if I'm about to miss my plane. Then I realize the announcement is not for my flight or airline, but I'm distracted nonetheless.

This moment is a microcosm of my life, and maybe of yours too. A constant barrage of noises, voices, and other input keeps me from hearing God's voice.

I try to focus on my writing. I shoot up a quick prayer asking God to help me block out the clatter so I can hear his voice and sense his leading. But the opposite happens. My ears pick up more than before: two boys arguing over a handheld video game, announcements by various airlines, and a man making an international call about a mix-up in a shipment. He is angry; I am frustrated!

Then in the midst of all of this, I hear God's voice reminding me to "be still and know that I am God." Through the chatter and clatter, he speaks to my heart. In that moment, I'm reminded that God breaks into the noisy and messy times with the same ease as during the quiet times of spiritual retreat.

Symptoms Check
I Am Hard of Hearing

☐ It irritates me when people talk about "hearing God speak."

☐ I would love to hear God speak but feel like I'm spiritually deaf.

☐ Sometimes I think I hear God speaking or sense his prompting, but I worry it's just my own ideas or my mind playing tricks on me.

☐ I make most of my decisions on my own, rarely seeking the wisdom of others.

☐ I have teams of people who give me their input and ideas, but if the truth be known, I gather these people so they will agree with me, not really to hear their input.

☐ I rarely ask friends for their perspective on my life and ministry.

Hearing God's Voice

In the days of Samuel, the word of the Lord was not often heard. God wanted to speak. He longed to communicate and commune with his people. But they refused. They rebelled. They were spiritually deaf. So it was thousands of years ago. So it is today. So it will ever be.

God is speaking. The question is, are we listening? His voice comes through every day. Loud and soft, overt and subtle, through the Spirit and through people, God is speaking. The trick is to learn to hear, to recognize, to listen, to respond.

Samuel was a young boy being raised in the house of the priest Eli, a servant of the Lord who was training Samuel to follow in his steps. Theirs is the story of a seasoned leader grooming the next generation to serve the Lord. Mentor and protégé.

One night a voice calls Samuel's name and awakens him. Naturally, he runs to find Eli, the only other person in the house. "Here I am; you called me." Eli seems a bit irritated. He sends Samuel back to bed. Again Samuel hears a voice and goes to Eli. Eli says, "My son, I did not call; go back and lie down," and sends him back to bed a second time.

At this point in the biblical account, we get a brief commentary: "Now Samuel did not yet know the Lord: The word of the Lord had not yet been revealed to him" (1 Sam. 3:7). This young boy had never heard God speak, but that would soon change! After Samuel goes back to bed and settles down, no doubt feeling a little confused and even scared, the voice speaks again. He hears his name, "Samuel." Once again he goes to the old prophet and asks if he has called.

Eli has an "ah ha" moment, realizing that God is speaking to Samuel. So Eli instructs him to go back and lay down one more time. But this time Eli gives Samuel simple, life-changing advice, godly counsel that all wise leaders should carry in their hearts. Eli tells Samuel that if he hears the voice again, he should say, "Speak, Lord, for your servant is listening" (v. 9).

This was the beginning of a new chapter in Samuel's life. The page turned and this young leader began a lifetime of waiting on God, listening for direction from a source much higher and greater than himself. Samuel learned that his leadership would have to flow from a deep personal connection with God, through ears that hear the voice of the Lord, or he would never become the leader he was destined to be.

"Speak, Lord, for your servant is listening." These words will transform a leader's life. Wise leaders are desperate to hear the voice of God. In a noisy world, our hearts should long for wisdom from above. Leaders need to receive direction, insight, and inspiration from God. As we cry out, "Speak, Lord, for your servant is listening," God will direct our steps.

Hearing and recognizing God's voice isn't just for the monastic or the zealot. It should be the normative daily experience of every Christian leader. Jesus, the Good Shepherd, makes it clear that his sheep recognize his voice. This is the only way they can follow him.

Self-Examination Suggestion
Listening for God's Voice

God speaks in the quiet times and also in the noisy flow of our days. As we learn to hear, recognize, and follow his voice in the calm places, we will become more attentive in the rushed times. Set aside thirty minutes and go where there will be no distractions. Bring a notebook for writing down impressions or words you receive from God. In this time, use the questions below to get you started, and add your own questions. After you ask each question, wait in silence. Ask God to speak to your heart and bring conviction or words of blessing. Listen attentively; say to God, "Speak, Lord, for your servant is listening."

1. How much do you love me, and how have you revealed this love?
2. Is there an area I need to grow in, and what step would you have me take?
3. Is there a person I need to serve, and what can I do to show your love?
4. What is one area of hidden sin in my life?
5. What word of blessing do you want me to give to someone?
6. Who do you want me to pray for, and what should I pray?

Help from My Friends
What Do You Do to Live an Examined Life?

Self-examination requires brutal honesty about yourself. Such honesty helps me admit I've drifted away from God, and why. When I feel emptiness and anxiety, I know that I am the one who moved. My very distance requires me to seek God out, as I know that I am avoiding him *because* of my disobedience. I can be an expert at denial when it comes to my inner life, but avoidance just prolongs the misery. An honest expression of my weakness and my sin quickly brings me back into God's presence. So when I recognize the signs, I stop and in prayerful confession seek his mercy and grace. He's always there. He never moves!

— Kim Levings, Director, Outreach Ministries

If you want to dig deeper into the topic of learning to hear and recognize God's voice, I suggest reading chapter 6 of my book *Seismic Shifts*. The chapter is titled "The Shift from Monologue to Dialogue," and it's all about how we can make conversational prayer a part of our spiritual journey.

Listening to the Generations

A wise leader longs to be challenged and stretched by people who have traveled farther down the leadership road. When we find people who have a wealth of experience to share, we can sit at their feet, listen, and learn. One of the best gifts we can give ourselves is finding a person or two who are older than we are and learning from them.

Every one of us has received the gift of proximity. God has placed people close to us, at various seasons of our lives, who can mentor and teach us. The question is, do we take time to listen? Are we humble enough to acknowledge that we don't have all of the answers? When God places a sage in our lives, it's for a reason.

I became a senior pastor for the first time when I came to Corinth Church. I was only thirty-one years old, but I was the "boss." The staff was a ten-hours-a-week secretary, a part-time choir director, a youth pastor, a custodial team, and a calling pastor. I was the lead pastor and the youngest member on the staff. The calling pastor was just shy of three times my age. Rev. John Schaal was in his eighties and was one of the most gentle, insightful, and powerful men I have ever known. He and his lovely wife, Grace, exuded the presence and tenderness of Jesus.

I still remember the first time it happened. I was at my desk early on a Sunday morning getting ready to preach. My door was closed because I was going my sermon notes one more time. Quietly the door opened and John came in. He didn't say a word; he just closed the door, walked very slowly across the room, and stood at my side. He lifted his frail hands and placed them on my head. Then he prayed. As this saint spoke with Jesus, I felt the power of heaven surge into my heart, my mind, my body. Tears flowed down my face. When he uttered the amen, he turned and walked out of my office.

I don't know how many times this happened over the next five years, but every time John came to pray for me, God showed up. I knew that I had to spend time with this man. Over the years, we had many lunches together. He never let me pay. I would always come with a couple of questions. We would order our food, I would ask a question, and then I would listen. Have you ever given a bowl of milk to a stray cat? That was me; I lapped up every drop! I tried to write down everything he said. It was gold.

Network Building
Finding Answers to Good Questions

Identify two or three wise people God has placed in proximity to you. They are there, if you take time to look around. Give them a call to see if you could spend a few hours asking questions and learning from them. Here are some of the questions I asked John when we met together. Feel free to use them, or make up your own.

- If you could preach on only one more text of the Bible, what would it be and why?
- When you visit people in the hospital, what passages do you read them?
- How did you meet your wife, and what have you done to build a marriage that has endured more than six decades of life and ministry?
- What are your favorite Old Testament and New Testament books?
- How have you maintained balance in your life and ministry?
- How have you handled conflict with people in the churches you have served?

I treasured the times I was able to be with John and just listen to him. He was a scholar, a pastor, and a model of a life surrendered to Jesus. When we began training seminary interns, we had them accompany John on his hospital visits and then have lunch with him. What a joy to see one generation passing the baton to the next. John was brokenhearted when he could no longer drive. But we had people drive him to visit the shut-ins from our congregation, and he was able to exercise his gifts into his mideighties. Even when he was bedridden, our church interns and staff members still went and sat with him — listening to, learning from, and loving this godly leader.

When John passed away, there were times early on Sunday mornings when I would sit at my desk reviewing my sermon notes and remember the weight of his hands on my head as he prayed for me. I still miss him, but the lessons he taught me are locked in my heart and mind. His influence is alive in my ministry.

If you and I were to have a conversation over a cup of coffee, I could tell you of others who have had a mentoring influence on my life. Dan Webster, my first youth pastor, birthed in me a passion to teach God's Word and gave me the opportunity to grow my teaching gift. Lois Van Haitsma (called Grandma Lois by all who know her) taught me the power of a hug and making time for words of kindness. Harold Korver mentored a whole group of young men and women as we went through seminary, and I have quoted his sage advice hundreds of times over the years. Kathryn Post, Emma Jerene Burgess, Dorothy Roosien, and Sherwin and Joan Vliem (my wife's parents) modeled lives of faithful prayer that have inspired and convicted me more times than I can recount. Each of these godly people has prayed for me and my family every single day for over thirteen years! I want to be more like them.

Wise leaders learn to identify people who have the experience of years of walking closely with Jesus. And when they get close to these people, they listen, ask good questions, watch, and learn. The best leaders know that the long journey of faithfulness and effectiveness is well-marked by others who have gone before them. None of us stands high enough to see the future with clarity. We need people in our lives who will stoop to lift us onto their spiritual shoulders.

I've Got Your Back

Find a Mentor

Who is mentoring you? This is what I have learned about mentors. They rarely come to you and say, "I am going to invest in your life." Most of the time we need to pray for God to bring someone into our lives, and then we have to take the initiative to meet with them and ask if they will walk with us. If you don't have a wise older leader investing in your life, don't waste time lamenting this fact; go and find a mentor. You will be amazed at how many people, with so much to offer, would love to pour into your life. I suggest meeting with this person no less than once a month, and more often if possible. Also, once you have established this relationship, let this person be a sounding board for leadership and life decisions. You will be blessed beyond measure.

Listening to Peers

Hubris runs deep in the lives of many leaders. We can be a proud lot who prefer solving problems and giving answers to asking others for their help. We can spend hours, weeks, months, and even years driving around a tough issue because we refuse to pull over and ask someone for directions. It is time for Christian leaders to humbly invite our peers who know more than we do to give us directions. What we are called to do with our lives is too important to waste any more time making U-turns on one-way streets and heading down the wrong road.

I must admit that left to my own devices, I tend to be prideful and self-sufficient. It's not natural for me to ask for directions, whether

I'm driving my car or on my leadership journey. But I have also felt the strong conviction of the Holy Spirit calling me to grow up, get over myself, and set pride aside. After trying the "I can do it by myself" route for about a decade, things began to change when I hit my thirties. The Spirit's voice broke through and I finally agreed to learn from my peers.

Help from My Friends

What Do You Do to Practice Self-Accountability?

Over the years, I have developed three simple tests I use when making decisions that involve my ethics and integrity. Each one is built around asking myself a specific question:

1. When I am making a decision that is in the gray area and not clearly black and white, I ask, "How would I feel about this being printed in our local newspaper for everyone to read?"

2. When making a decision about a person's raise or bonus, I ask, "If I inadvertently left this information on my desk and other staff members saw it, would I feel comfortable explaining the differences in raises and bonuses that each person was to receive so they could understand why their amount was more or less than someone else's?"

3. There always seem to be more demands for our time than there is time available. After necessary business relationships, I try to prioritize who to spend time with and how much time to spend. One of the questions I ask myself to help me decide is, "Will this person be at my 85th birthday party?" If the answer is yes, I take all the time I can and then some. If not, I spend the time that is necessary and proper and move on.

— Bruce Ryskamp, President and CEO, Zondervan (1993–2005)

At that time, I developed a discipline of creating self-directed study experiences to sharpen my mind and develop my leadership abilities. I decided I would identify colleagues in ministry who (dare I say it?) know more than I do and learn from them. Over the years, I have done this by calling other leaders, telling them that I believe they have something to offer me, and asking if I can spend some time learning from them. From pastors to business leaders to corporate CEOs, many have said yes.

I have learned that I need these experiences to sharpen me in areas in which God wants to expand my mind. When I identify an area I need to grow in, I look for people in my geographical area who are experts or are well ahead of me in their knowledge, and who I feel will be effective in teaching me. I then set personal learning goals and contact them. In effect, I've placed myself in an ongoing, advanced-study program that costs me only the price of lunches and has led to a number of lasting friendships and partnerships in ministry.

A few years ago, I was moving into a new leadership role. We were going to add an executive pastor position (Pastor of Church Ministries was the title we used), and I was going to hand over many of the responsibilities I had carried as senior pastor. The church had never developed a role like this, and I had never worked with an executive pastor, so I called three churches in our area that were already using this model effectively. I asked each of the lead pastors if they would give me an extended lunch time so I could learn from them and from the model used by their church. They all said yes!

Over the next couple of weeks, I met with Wayne Schmidt (pastor of Kentwood Community Church, a Wesleyan congregation), Frank Weaver (pastor of Calvary Christian Reformed Church), and Rob Bell (pastor of Mars Hill Bible Church). In each case, I asked specific questions about how their leadership model was working. I studied their lines of accountability and their division of responsibilities. Each had strengths and weaknesses. When it was all said and done, I learned from each leader and congregation. I was humbled that these leaders would carve out part of their day to teach me and be a blessing to the church I serve. And I was struck by the reality that each of these leaders has a kingdom heart that extends well beyond their own churches.

After these meetings, I synthesized what I learned and worked with my team to create a model that drew from the strengths of these other examples and avoided the pitfalls they had experienced. (Each leader had honestly shared the weaknesses in their structures, which helped us avoid making some of the same mistakes.) After our staff team had developed our model, I sent a copy of our work and vision to the three leaders and shared how they had helped me and my church to be more effective. One of the leaders sent back a note and told me that they were going to begin shaping their leadership structures more like our model; he thought it would better serve their church.

As a wonderful side note to this little study, Wayne Schmidt has became a dear friend. Over the years, we have met periodically to learn from each other. Wayne, a skilled high-level leader, has been a leadership mentor. And I have shared with him what I know about mobilizing a church to move into the community with the message of God's love. Since our first meeting, we have had many lunches, and I have preached at his church, led devotions for his staff, and helped with some evangelism training. Whenever we meet, iron sharpens iron, and both of us are encouraged.

Network Building
Learning from Peers

Make a list of leaders you respect who work within a hundred miles of where you live. What might you learn if you were to spend a few hours with these people? What questions might you ask? How might God sharpen you as a leader through spending time with them? Write down the questions you would ask if you had a couple of hours to spend with each of them. Identify specific areas you believe they could help you grow in. Then call them. Ask if they would be willing to spend a couple of hours to invest in your life and ministry. Many will say yes. If someone is too busy, don't feel bad; just move to the next person on your list.

Let's be honest, we don't have all of the answers. And we don't have to reinvent the wheel every time we want to go somewhere. God has placed people all around us who have a great deal to offer. I have discovered that most are more than willing to share their wisdom, expertise, and even failings if asked.

Listening to Friends

Some time ago I had to make a number of decisions that would impact my ministry, personal life, and family. One part of the decision-making process had business and financial implications that were well beyond my understanding. The truth is, I don't care very much about financial stuff. But I knew what I had to do. I gathered with some of the members of the Country Club of Hudsonville (CCH) so I could pick their brains, ask questions, and learn from their wisdom. The CCH is actually a warehouse where a friend has a virtual golf machine. During the long, cold, snowy, cloudy, icy, sleety, occasionally depressing Michigan winter months, we gather to hit golf balls against images of warmer and greener places projected on a big screen. In these times together, we talk, laugh, and seek to maintain our sanity.

These friends are business leaders. They are all insightful. They all care about each other. And when it comes to business and financial savvy, they can run laps around me. One evening, as we hit balls and talked, I asked the group, "Can we spend some time focusing on me? Would all of you give me your insight on some key decisions I need to make?" They were more than willing. Ron, Brad, Harold, and Gary listened as I explained what I was facing and the options I had. None of them gave immediate advice but picked my brain for over an hour. They asked questions. They processed the data. Then they shared insights that were solid gold.

They pressed me to think about things that had not even crossed my mind. They drew out implications I had missed. Because they stood at a different vantage point, they helped me see through a fresh set of eyes. Honestly, I was a little embarrassed. They saw things that made perfect sense to them that I had missed. But they didn't make me feel stupid or belittle me. They simply gave me a perspective I lacked. Because of their input, I made a series of decisions that were far wiser than if I had tried to figure things out on my own.

Network Building
Help from My Friends

The members of the CCH also travel together on occasion. The leader of this informal network is Ron Vander Pol. Ron is a gifted businessman who has a unique ability to bridge relational connections that have great kingdom impact. He also loves to challenge leaders to think in new ways. When we are going to travel together, Ron will occasionally give us a homework assignment. He picks a book, usually one that will stir the pot, and gives us each a copy. We are to read the book and make it a point of conversation on the trip.

In the summer of 2006, we went to the West Coast for a long weekend. Our text for reading and discussion was Al Gore's book on global warming, *An Inconvenient Truth*. The book sparked many conversations as well as hours of bantering as we sat by a roaring fire in the evening hours and challenged each other's ideas and preconceived notions. We didn't solve all of the ecological problems facing our world. But we were all stirred by the profound reality that the God who made the heavens and earth still cares about his creation, and so should we.

A surprising benefit came out of this learning process. Ron asked me to lead a worship service and bring a message on the Sunday evening of our trip. My message was "Inconvenient Truths from the Sermon on the Mount." We gathered outdoors around a fire and spent time praying, talking, and grappling with Jesus' challenging and unsettling words. This one sermon later developed into a series of messages I taught on a university campus.

I find that having a group of friends who aren't part of my church is very valuable. And building friendships with business leaders has been a blessing and a joy. I learn much as they talk about the corporate world and how leadership works in their contexts. Each of us has a circle of friends who can offer wisdom and insight. Their vantage point might be exactly what we need in our lives or ministries.

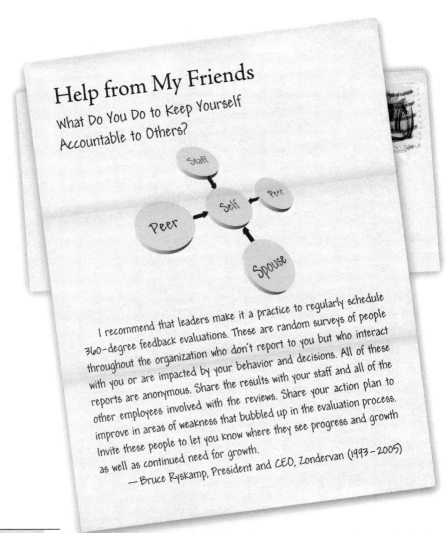

Help from My Friends

What Do You Do to Keep Yourself Accountable to Others?

I recommend that leaders make it a practice to regularly schedule 360-degree feedback evaluations. These are random surveys of people throughout the organization who don't report to you but who interact with you or are impacted by your behavior and decisions. All of these reports are anonymous. Share the results with your staff and all of the other employees involved with the reviews. Share your action plan to improve in areas of weakness that bubbled up in the evaluation process. Invite these people to let you know where they see progress and growth as well as continued need for growth.

— Bruce Ryskamp, President and CEO, Zondervan (1993 – 2005)

Hearing Concerns and Critique

Leaders in Christian ministry will be criticized, critiqued, and evaluated ... constantly. It's part of the deal. The key is learning to recognize unhealthy criticism and ignore it. At the same time, we must know how to identify helpful critique and listen so we can learn. I learned this lesson as a teenager when I was volunteering in a youth ministry in Garden Grove, California.

I had been serving in the church high school ministry for just over a year. I loved it! It had become my passion. Though I was still a senior in high school, I had been asked to be a campus leader and was doing some teaching under the mentorship of our youth pastor. I knew in my heart that this was training for a lifetime in ministry. I could feel the Holy Spirit working through me. I was having the time of my life.

One of the key leaders of the ministry called to see if I could meet with him. I was so excited. What new area of responsibility or challenge might I be facing? What affirmation might I hear for my passionate and faithful sacrifice of close to twenty hours of volunteer ministry each week?

We sat on the grass by the church administration offices. I looked at this godly leader whom I respected so much. He was high energy, articulate about his faith, a leader of leaders, and he had the biggest afro I had ever seen on a white guy. What wasn't there to respect? I was ready to receive Yoda-like insight from this great leader.

He looked me in the eye and said, "Kevin, you have a problem with pride. We are going to remove you from your ministry position so you can work on this weak point in your character."

I got fired! That's right, I got released from a volunteer job. It's bad enough to get fired from a real paying job, but this was just plain humiliating.

My appreciation for and awe of this man melted away instantly. I thought to myself (and I'll give you the PG-rated version), "Are you firing me? I'm a volunteer! Who are you to talk about my having a pride problem; you are one of the cockiest guys I have ever met! You can take your advice and this volunteer ministry position and ..." Suffice it to say, I was angry.

My mind was reeling, but thankfully I had the restraint to keep my mouth shut. I listened. I pondered his words. Sure, I was outraged, but as I sat there in stunned silence, the truth sank in. Waves of emotion hit me: first was rage, then shock, then defensiveness, then a strange and peaceful calm.

He was right!

As I looked at this bearer of bad news, his monstrous afro swaying in the breeze, I was certain he had a very similar pattern of pride in his life. But the Holy Spirit hit me over the head with a simple, painful, and deeply needed word. I had a problem and it was making me ineffective in ministry. Pride was ruling my heart. God helped me look past the messenger and listen to the message.

Over the years, God has graciously brought people into my life who have spoken truth I needed to hear. Sometimes they have been gentle people who love me and come with great sensitivity. At other times the message has come with sharp edges and the bearer has been harsh and mean-spirited. But when I have sensed that the critique is valid and the word is from the Lord, I have tried, with all my strength, to receive it.

Help from My Friends
What Do You Do to Keep Yourself Accountable to Others?

I learned many years ago that I shouldn't *expect* of myself anything that I wasn't willing to *inspect*. This became a foundational principle for me. If my goal is to lead a godly life in which people see Christ in how I behave, the decisions I make, and how I treat others, it is necessary for me to receive honest feedback on how others perceive my performance.

Through the years (in both my work life and home life), I have deliberately set up "feedback channels" with the people I interact with and who are impacted by my leadership. How do I do that?

When you are in leadership, it is very difficult to get truthful feedback from the people you lead. Through the years, I've developed some guidelines to help me get honest feedback:

1. Let people know that you expect them to give honest feedback.

2. Encourage accountability by publicly rewarding people for correcting you and calling you to be accountable for your behavior.

3. Never defend or explain your actions or behavior at the time you are receiving criticism from someone you lead. Remember, it was probably very difficult for them to come to you and give you criticism. If you do, they will probably never take this risk again and they will most likely warn their friends also. Instead, thank them and let them know you realize how much courage it took for them to come to you and that you appreciate their feedback. They will tell others about this, and it will encourage others to give you feedback in the future.

— Bruce Ryskamp, President and CEO, Zondervan (1993–2005)

Of course, there have also been times when someone has come with criticism that was unfounded, overstated, or just plain malicious. I have had to discern when this is the case and disregard those attacks. The key is learning to receive God-sent messages through others and knowing when to ignore ungodly attacks.

God still speaks.

Samuel learned to recognize God's voice, and he was never the same. He said, "Speak Lord, your servant is listening," and the Lord revealed his will. Sheep recognize the voice of their shepherd and they follow. If we are going to lead effectively in a complex and confusing world, learning to listen is essential.

God is speaking through the gentle voice of his Spirit, through wise leaders who have gone before us, through effective leaders all around us, through brothers and sisters who love us, through those who lead us, and through those we are called to lead.

God is speaking ... listen.

chapter 4

Clear Vision Sees What Lies Ahead

The Leader's Eyes

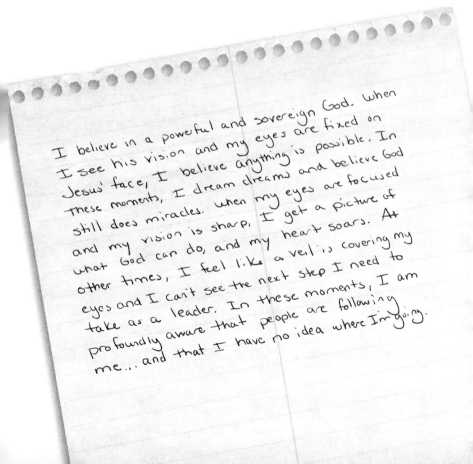

I believe in a powerful and sovereign God. When I see his vision and my eyes are fixed on Jesus' face, I believe anything is possible. In these moments, I dream dreams and believe God still does miracles. When my eyes are focused and my vision is sharp, I get a picture of what God can do, and my heart soars. At other times, I feel like a veil is covering my eyes and I can't see the next step I need to take as a leader. In these moments, I am profoundly aware that people are following me... and that I have no idea where I'm going.

> When the servant of the man of God got up and went out early the next morning, an army with horses and chariots had surrounded the city. "Oh, my lord, what shall we do?" the servant asked. "Don't be afraid," the prophet answered. "Those who are with us are more than those who are with them." And Elisha prayed, "O LORD, open his eyes so he may see." Then the LORD opened the servant's eyes, and he looked and saw the hills full of horses and chariots of fire all around Elisha.
>
> —2 Kings 6:15–17

Leaders need to have sharp eyes to see culture as it is, to see the intricacies of human relationships, and to see what lies on the horizon. But even more important, leaders need to see the presence of God. When we open our eyes to the spiritual reality around us, everything else snaps into focus.

Elisha, Elijah's protégé, knew this. In 2 Kings 6:8, we enter the drama. The king of Aram has Elisha in his sights. He wants him dead. It seems that Elisha has been involved in insider trading. God has been giving Elisha details about the political and military plans of the Arameans (the enemies of Israel), and Elisha has been feeding this sensitive information to Israel's king.

Now the army of the Arameans has surrounded the city of Dothan, where Elisha and his servant had stayed for the night. When they walk out in the morning, Elisha's servant just about wets himself. He sees a huge military force surrounding the city, and he knows why they are there. No doubt a simple reality is passing through his mind: "We are dead men!"

The servant glances at the prophet. Elisha's countenance is peaceful and calm—irritatingly so! It's as if he has no idea of the peril they are facing. So the servant speaks, "Oh, my lord, what shall we do?" You can almost hear the panic in his voice.

Elisha's response sounds like madness to the uninitiated. Although the servant has seen many miracles and knows the Spirit of God is on Elisha, he feels this particular situation will lead to his and Elisha's demise. He has seen Elisha provide oil for a widow, supply bread for a hundred men, cleanse leprosy, and even raise a dead boy. But this is different. They are surrounded by an army of seasoned soldiers. They are trapped.

Calmly Elisha says, "Don't be afraid. Those who are with us are more than those who are with them." The servant strains his eyes, trying to see some great army in the distance coming to save the day. All he can see is a wall of enemy soldiers with swords and spears in hand. Then comes the prayer, one we must pay close attention to. Elisha cries out to God, "O LORD, open his eyes so he may see."

At this moment, Elisha's servant enters a whole new reality, the place where Elisha lives every day. He sees behind the veil and his courage quotient jumps about a hundred times. The enemy is still there. The army of the Arameans is posted with weapons and superior numbers. But surrounding them is the army of God. The hills are filled with horses and chariots of fire. God is present. He who is with us is greater than those who are against us. He can see it all.

Fear is dispelled. Hope is born. Confidence runs rampant.

Do you want to help your ministry press into enemy territory and accomplish great things for the kingdom of God? Begin to pray, with faith and confidence, "Open my eyes, Lord, that I may see!" This prayer is not about seeing culture or ministry strategies, as important as these things may be. It is about having the veil pulled back and your eyes opened to see the presence of the spiritual world.

As leaders, it can be easy to take a posture of fear-filled defeat. We see only the obstacles and are paralyzed. Our eyes are fixed on all the wrong things: the world is too powerful to overcome, denominational structures stand in the way, resources are scarce, and people are resistant. We just don't know if we have the energy to face one more leadership challenge.

Then we pray, "Lord, open my eyes that I may see." As we cry out for God's vision and perspective, we see the hand of God reach out, take hold of the veil of eternity, and pull it back. We see the horses and chariots of fire. Our eyes behold the presence of the Holy Spirit. We see angelic messengers coming from the throne of the Mighty One. Our hope rises, our courage is renewed, our vision is restored. In these moments, we become a whole new kind of leader.

Symptoms Check

My Vision Is Poor

☐ I see obstacles much more clearly than the vision of God that surmounts all obstacles.

☐ I know there is a spiritual world all around me, but I have no idea how to see and discern what is happening in this world of the spirit.

☐ I have moments when I feel God is giving me a vision of what he might want to do in my life and ministry, but I push them aside and focus on what is practical, acceptable, expected, and safe.

☐ My eyes are always focused on the future, and I have a hard time looking back and learning from the past.

Seeing behind the Veil

Elisha's servant had a defining moment. When he woke up that morning, he had lived his whole life seeing only what his eyes could see. When he went to bed that night, he had visions of chariots of fire. He had seen behind the veil into the spiritual world, and he would never be the same.

How is your vision? Do you see with more than your physical eyes? Are you aware, day by day, of the spiritual world that exists all around you? Do you sense the presence of God? Do you see the Spirit at work in your daily activities? Are you aware of the spiritual battles raging in the heavenly realms and in your church?

The apostle Paul writes, "Finally, be strong in the Lord and in his mighty power. Put on the full armor of God so that you can

Help from My Friends
How Do You Guard Your Heart?

As a leader of a larger church, I realize I am a target for the Evil One. As a sinful person, I am a big target. What helps is brutal honesty within my own heart, and transparency with a couple of guy buddies in the church. I like to have periodic spiritual gut checks. I ask myself hard questions such as:

- Am I speaking or responding out of pride?
- Am I cutting someone down with my words or actions?
- Am I complaining because I seek attention?

These honest internal conversations really help. I have also given two close friends (elders in my church) freedom 24/7 to speak truth into my life. They can ask me anything. It's tough, but it works. They ask me questions about my motives in meetings, attitudes toward people, my purity in relationship to women, and anything else they think needs examination.

— Bob Bouwer, Senior Pastor, Faith Church, Dyer, IN

take your stand against the devil's schemes. For our struggle is not against flesh and blood, but against the rulers, against the authorities, against the powers of this dark world and against the spiritual forces of evil in the heavenly realms" (Eph. 6:10–12). He goes on to describe the various pieces of armor that will help us stand strong against the enemy. This passage, along with so many others, reminds us that our leadership is not just about setting goals, delivering messages, running an organization, and keeping people happy. Christian leaders are called to enter this battle. In the name and power of the resurrected Christ, we are to lead the church to the very gates of hell and kick them in (Matt. 16:18). We are to seek and save those who are lost (Luke 15). We are to resist the devil and watch him flee (James 4:7). We are to wage war with heavenly weapons that will demolish strongholds (2 Cor. 10:4). If we are going to enter this battlefield and lead the people of God to victory, our eyes must be fixed on Jesus.

I've Got Your Back
The Power of Discernment

People with the spiritual gift of discernment are gifts to the church and to leaders who will learn from them. They know when the enemy is at work. They can discern when human motives are inconsistent with the heart of God. Those who have this biblical (1 Cor. 12:10) spiritual gift and have developed it have the ability to bring a word of warning and even conviction to other Christians.

I don't have this gift, but I know a few people who do. Over the years, these people have challenged attitudes, motives, or actions in my life that did not honor God. In some cases, I had worked very hard to keep these things hidden and felt like only God and I knew about them. I was wrong! God had pulled back the veil and given spiritual eyesight to a brother or sister who came to me and called me out.

For many years, I was bothered by this. Then I realized that I need people around me who can see hidden areas of sin in my life, areas sometimes I don't even notice myself. Brothers and sisters with the gift of discernment cover my back on a whole new level, and I have learned to give them permission to speak into my life. Quite honestly, I still tend to get defensive and resist what they say ... at first. But with time, my heart softens and I receive their warning or words of conviction.

Every leader has people in their ministry who have the gift of discernment. We are both courageous and wise when we seek them out and invite them to speak into our lives. If you feel led to do this, make sure you let those people know that you will be on a learning curve and that you might be a little cranky or defensive when they first bring concerns to you. Also remember that they are fallible and that you will need to seek the Lord to confirm the word of warning they give you.

The Wisdom of the Past

Leaders are visionaries. They tend to look forward, aspiring to what is next, not lingering on the past. Sometimes we are forward-looking to our own peril. Wise leaders discover the wealth of wisdom from the past. They stop, make a 180 degree turn, and slowly observe where they have been and where the church has been. They learn from, even celebrate, the past.

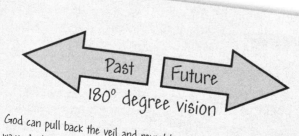

Past | Future

180° degree vision

God can pull back the veil and reveal his presence and will in many ways. As leaders, we learn to look back to learn from the past, look around to see what God is doing now, and look ahead to seek his vision for the future.

Doctor's Insight
Knowing Your Family History

Over the years, I've had a number of doctors. The first time I meet with a new doctor, I'm asked a whole battery of questions. One of the categories is family history. The doctor asks questions like, "Do you have a history of heart disease in your family?" If you do, he or she pays special attention to your heart. In the family-history part of the interview, there are always questions about smoking, drinking, and drug use. At this point I always talk about the history of alcoholism in my family. I became aware of this history when my Granny sat me down when I was fourteen years old and told me about the damage alcoholism has caused our family for many generations.

At this point, every doctor gives me a stern warning to be "very, very careful" when it comes to drinking. Because of my family history, I am predisposed, on many levels, to become a problem drinker. I have always heeded my doctors' warnings.

Leaders who want to stay healthy in their ministry will discover the wisdom of knowing their family history. This is true in our personal lives. We can avoid generational sin and dysfunction if we are aware of them and take measures to live in a different way. The harmful decisions of past generations do not have to dictate our future. In a similar way, leaders who know the family history of their church can avoid past patterns and pitfalls. Good leaders are good historians.

In my first few years of ministry, I spent about 99.9 percent of my time pressing forward. I was all about what's next. I had no idea that

God was building the church of today on a foundation established over years, decades, and centuries.

Then, thankfully, I met Harold Korver, the pastor of a dynamic and community-transforming church in Paramount, California. He was also the father of a close friend I met in seminary. To top it all off, Harold informally mentored a number of us "visionary," "high-powered," "forward-looking" leaders. He was a gift placed in our lives by a loving and gracious God who knew we needed a voice inviting us to look back as we pressed forward.

One day while we were conversing, Harold said something that cut into my soul and marked me for life. He was talking about leading a church that had generations of history. Harold said, "Bless their past, and they will bless your future. Damn their past, and they will damn your future." I did not absorb the full weight of this statement until I became the senior pastor of a church that was celebrating their hundredth anniversary on the very Sunday I began my ministry.

Corinth Church in Byron Center, Michigan, had generations of history under its belt before I showed up on the scene. This church had been faithfully serving Jesus for many decades before I was even born. As I started my ministry, my natural tendency was to press forward. But Pastor Korver's words rang in my ears and were alive in my heart. So I studied the history of the church. Where and when had God done great things? Who were the pastors God had called to influence this congregation over the years? I walked down the hallway near the church offices and looked at the row of photographs of pastors who had led the church over the past century. I studied their faces, their eyes. I thanked God for these men.

As I reflected on the past and tried to learn from the former pastors' mistakes and victories, I was stirred to do something. I found out which pastors were still living, and I wrote each of them a personal note. I thanked them for their leadership, courage, love for the church, and the unique contributions God had led them to make. I asked for their prayers as I led in this next season. I sought to bless them and what God had done in the past. I heard back from some of these leaders and was struck by how much it meant for them to receive words of blessing and to be invited into the role of prayer support in the next season of the church's ministry.

Network Building
Blessing the Past

If the church you serve has been around for a while, learn its history—the good, the bad, and the ugly. Also, if there are pastors who served before you, consider blessing them in some way and invite them to pray for you and the church. Allow them to be partners in the next season.

I can still remember sending a note to one of the previous pastors of Corinth Church, James Goldschmeding. Jim was called to lead in a tough time of transition. His role was breaking up the hard ground, bringing a strong challenge to consider changing worship styles, and moving the heart of the church outward. He served in a time of tilling, planting, and watering. But he did not get to stay for the harvest. When I came, the church was ready for a season of ingathering. When I wrote to Jim and later talked to him face-to-face, I told him that his faithful service and strong leadership had prepared the church for a time of growth and spiritual harvest. He was able to share in the joy of the great work God was doing and was reminded that his hard season was a big part of the present harvest.

I was also moved to bless the past as often as I could from the pulpit. This church was filled with people whose families had been part of the congregation going back a full hundred years. I spoke of the courage and faith of these dear people who had sacrificed to build a little church in the middle of nowhere. I celebrated their tenacity for keeping the church alive even when the railroad, which was suppose to go right by the church, was diverted a number of miles south to the teeming metropolis of Moline (population 219). I often reminded the congregation of the faith they exhibited for many years before I led the church. Just a few years before I came, the church had purchased eighteen acres of land and had built a worship center that was almost three times larger than the congregation. I reminded them that they were either incredibly visionary or just plain irresponsible.

The closer I looked, the more there was to celebrate. I can still remember the Sunday morning about two years into my ministry at Corinth when I asked all those who had been part of the church when they built the new worship center to stand up. I thanked these people for having the vision to make space for new people. I blessed them for counting the cost and believing in God. Before they could sit down, spontaneously all those seated began to applaud. You see, there were almost as many "new people" as there were long-term members. Many of those who had come to the church over the past two years were new believers. Their unprompted vigorous applause said it all. They were expressing thanks for past faithfulness.

The Eyes of Wisdom

Early in my ministry at Corinth, I recognized that learning from the past is mandatory for a ministry's healthy future. I began to call on some of the leaders who had made a significant impact on the church in the past. I wanted to learn by looking back, but my vantage point was fairly limited.

I needed help, so I made a list of people I thought could teach me. First on my list was Warren Burgess. He had grown up in the small community of Byron Center and was a son of the church. He had become a pastor and had led a number of churches with great effectiveness. Upon his retirement, Warren moved back into the community. I quickly connected with him and asked if he would be willing to offer his advice and perspective when I felt it was needed. After a short time, he came on the church staff part-time to lead our ministry to those in the hospital and to the shut-ins. He recruited and trained an amazing team of church members who minister with compassion to those in the church facing times of need. Countless times over the next decade, I went to Warren for insight, prayer, and wisdom.

Something glorious emerged from this ministry partnership. His love for Jesus, his gentle spirit, and his godly authority impacted a whole group in the church. Those who were over fifty and somewhat weary of the "new things" and "strange changes" had a deep respect for Warren. When he said, "I support what God is doing at Corinth," these folks were more open to getting on board. It made a huge impact when Warren stood in front of the congregation and blessed the other pastors and our leadership. The voice of the past blessed the future, and we experienced unity rather than civil war.

I've Got Your Back

Know Your History

If you don't have a strong grasp of the history of the church you serve, gather the local historians. There is always a group of people who know and love the history of the church. Gather a few of them for coffee and ask them to tell the story. If this process is helpful and the group offers good insight, consider asking them to do three things:

- Pray for the next season of the church's history to honor God and bless people.
- Be available if you need them as a sounding board for how future decisions might impact those with a long history in the church.
- Bless where God is taking the church in the future as a way of honoring the past.

I praise God that Harold Korver had the courage to speak these words to a group of emerging leaders: "Bless their past, and they will bless your future. Damn their past, and they will damn your future." Too many of us focus solely on the future and forget to learn from, remember, and bless the past. As our eyes are turned back, we discover much about where God wants to take us tomorrow.

Look Around and Notice Where God Is at Work

The first time I walked with a group through Henry Blackaby's *Experiencing God* curriculum, I was staggered by the simplicity of his message. Look around, see where God is at work, and join in! Over and over Henry tells stories of how this straightforward approach transformed a life or a church.

I will not try to duplicate what Henry teaches but will direct you to his signature work, *Experiencing God*, and his many other books on looking around and entering the flow of what God is doing. I encourage every church leadership team to go through these materials. Over the course of more than a decade, the leadership team at Corinth has sought to slow down, look around, and notice where God is at work. Every time we have done this, noticed a clear movement of God's Spirit, and joined in, good things have happened.

In the midnineties, we could see that the church was growing and God was bringing lots of young families in. Little kids were everywhere, the nursery was exploding, and there were many more on the way. Maybe it didn't take great spiritual discernment, but we identified that we needed to develop our children's ministry. For about a hundred and four years, we had operated the children's department with only volunteers. I knew it would be a stretch to get many of the church members to see the need to add a children's director to our staff. "We have done a fine job without a staff person for a hundred years" would be the battle cry.

Knowing it might be a tough sell, the staff and church board proposed that we add a part-time strategic staff person to take the role of "equipping the saints for the work of ministry" to our children. The search team found a woman in the church who had a college degree in education, had a seminary degree in theology and spiritual formation, and was married to the senior pastor. They offered my wife, Sherry, the position. She prayed about it and accepted.

Eight years later, she was leading a staff of five, and this team was overseeing about two hundred volunteers who led the ministry to children from nursery to fourth grade. At that time, the children's department, including children and volunteers, was larger than the entire church was when we added this position. Eight years earlier, we looked around and saw where God was at work. We dared to enter in and trust, by faith, that God would lead us forward. And the lives of hundreds of children have been impacted in glorious ways.

Another example of looking around and seeing what God is doing at Corinth Church began over a decade ago and continues today. The members of the church have always had a passion to share the message of Jesus with people in their community and all the way to the ends of the earth. For the first hundred years of the church's history, they did this primarily through sending money to missionaries overseas. Like many other churches, Corinth had a heart to reach out but did not know what steps to take beyond traditional mission support.

As I began my pastoral ministry at the church, I made it clear that one of our primary areas of focus would be evangelism. The church had expressed its commitment to fulfilling the Great Commission, and we agreed that this would be a significant emphasis in the years to come. The church members had always believed in the call to reach out. They had always wanted to take action. Now was the time. Hearts were right, the commitment was public, and we were ready to move into the harvest fields.

Over the following years, we developed an outreach team that partnered with all of the church ministries. We became more intentional about supporting overseas missions but also actually sent teams into the mission field, including to Kenya to do AIDs work, to Mexico to work with people in poverty, to New Orleans for hurricane relief, to the Netherlands to lead worship and street evangelism, to Egypt to partner with a church developing its facilities, and to the Caribbean to rebuild a school. At the same time, the church engaged in over thirty local outreach ministries, trained over two-thousand believers in personal evangelism, and saw hundreds come to faith in our own community.

We saw God at work, stirring hearts and calling us forward. But the church had to take steps to reach out with God's love. Here is one amazing figure. Before we wholeheartedly committed to making Corinth Church an evangelism center, our church budget was $240,000 a year. Today the outreach budget for local and world evangelism is over a quarter of a million dollars. Again, as we looked around and saw God at work, as we entered in, God showed up and did amazing things.

Healthy leaders look back to learn from the past; they also know how to read the times and see what God is doing now. And leaders seek the wisdom of the Spirit as they look ahead and follow God into the future.

Developing a God-Honoring Vision

After my first year as the lead pastor at Corinth Church, we formed a long-range planning team representing a cross section of the church: young and old, men and women, long-time members and new people. This team was to work with the pastors as we set goals for the next one to two years, three to five years, and six to ten years. In a century of ministry, the church had never done this kind of vision casting.

About two months into the process, we ran full speed into a parked trash truck. There it was, right in the middle of the road, and we were not proceeding until we dealt with it. The problem surfaced as people on the planning team began to make comments like, "We won't accomplish any long-range goals because the pastor will leave in a couple of years," and, "Why set these kinds of goals? The next pastor will just lead us in a different direction." I was a little hurt when I realized that most of the people on this creative dream team (some of the cream of the crop in the church) didn't think I would stick around for more than a few years.

Then I took a walk down the church hallway and looked at the pictures of my pastoral predecessors. I studied the small gold plates below their faces and was struck by the reality that the average pastor had stayed at the church for only three or four years. The people were simply responding to their experience over the decades. They had good reason to expect that I would have a short tenure.

I, on the other hand, felt the clear call of God to plan for the future and seek God's vision for an extended season of ministry. How would these two colliding perceptions be resolved?

After I told Sherry about the dilemma, we committed to a season of intense prayer. We would pray for God to lead us and speak to us about our ministry. We invited the church leaders and our couples small group to support us in this time of seeking God's leading and will for our lives. After about two months, the answer came clearly as God spoke to both me and Sherry. We were to make a ten-year commitment to Corinth Church.

We announced to the church board, the staff, the long-range planning team, and then to the congregation that we would be serving Corinth Reformed Church for no less than ten years. As fast as you can snap your fingers, the huge trash truck square in the middle of the road was towed away, and we moved forward. It surprised me that no one in the church questioned that we had heard the Lord and that our commitment was sincere. They took us at our word and were ready to follow.

Self-Examination Suggestion
Stepping Stone or Kingdom Commitment?

Evaluate your commitment to your present ministry. Do you see this place as a stepping stone to bigger and better things, or as God's kingdom assignment for you? Sometimes God's assignment can be short-term, but I grow more and more convicted that churches need leaders who are committed for the long haul. It is hard to lead a church if the people know you will be packing shortly after you've settled in. If you see your place of service as a stepping stone to a better job, ask the Spirit to speak to your heart about this. If you believe you are right where God wants you, consider praying about committing to long-term ministry in this place.

Over the next two years, the church gobbled up the one- to two-year goals and also engaged in all of the three- to five-year goals. We moved from one morning service to two. We shifted from a traditional style and order of worship that had not been seriously altered for a hundred years and introduced new music and creative elements to the service. We built a ministry training center that allowed us to expand our youth ministry as well as become a regional training hub. We added another full-time pastor. We also purchased another fifteen acres of land.

I still remember the night the long-range planning team presented their ten-year vision. I thought it was too aggressive. I felt they were asking for too much. I loved all of the ideas and knew God could accomplish all of these things, but I didn't think the church would buy in. Not only did the church get the vision but it unleashed the full fury of its prayers, generosity, and Midwest work ethic on it.

When the ten-year period came to a close, many worried that I would be packing to move. But God called me, Sherry, and our boys to continued ministry at Corinth. Over the next couple of years, I continued as the senior pastor, transferring much of my leadership role to Don Porter, the pastor we brought on to fulfill one of the church's three- to five-year goals.

Then when it seemed like the right time, with the blessing and leadership of the church board, Don took the reins as the lead pastor and I became the teaching pastor. For a year and a half, I stayed in this role and continued a glorious season of ministry at Corinth in the areas of preaching and evangelism. Then, with great clarity, God called me to conclude my ministry at Corinth Church at the start of 2007.

In the fall of 2006, Sherry and I sat with Don and Beth Porter and shared, with broken hearts, that our ministry at Corinth was coming to a close. You have to understand that words can't express the love we have for this body of believers. Our lives have been shaped by them in ways we don't fully understand. When we came to the church, our boys were six, four, and two. Now they are young men. Most of our adult lives have been invested in building a biblical church community in the greater Grand Rapids area. We did not want to leave. When I concluded my ministry at Corinth, the church was in a time of health, unity, and fruitfulness unparalleled in its one-hundred-and-fourteen-year history. And to top it off, as I transitioned out, a new team was setting a series of new goals for the next season of ministry.

Casting a Vision for the Next Chapter

After more than thirteen years of leading the board meetings at Corinth Church, I came to my last meeting. With almost a hundred and sixty meetings behind me, I had one last chance to speak into the board members' lives. I looked at this group of leaders and gave them a final exhortation: follow God's vision. I then shared how I believe they will know when they are on track. My list was not exhaustive and simply was intended to help them judge whether they are on the right course. I close this chapter with three statements about the vision of the church that I hope inspire you to evaluate your church's vision.

> 1. *God's vision will always be bigger than you can manage on your own.* I assured them that if they pulled in the reins on the ministry and did only what they could manage on their own, they could be confident that God would not be in it. God wants us to be in over our heads, so that we are driven to our knees in prayer, forced to trust in him alone, and so that all the glory goes to him. When we follow God's vision for our lives and ministries, we can be certain that there is no way our energy, creativity, or passion could have accomplished the great things that result. We declare, "Only God!" and give him the glory.
>
> 2. *God's vision will always cost us more than we think we can give*, and it will drive leaders to call others to sacrifice more than they feel is possible. We are called to a cross, to offer our whole bodies as living sacrifices, to place everything on the altar. We can know we are on track with God's vision when we have poured out all we think we have, and then hear a call to give even more.

3. *God's vision will always drive us toward the needs of the world and the hearts of the lost.* Whatever ministry we are in, God always moves his people out, in growing measure, toward those who are broken, lonely, lost, and needy. If we are pressing into new territory and reaching the lost, we are on the right track.

chapter 5

Affirming Words Bring Blessing and Energy

The Leader's Mouth

I know my words really matter. I am a leader in Christ's church, and what I say can bring healing or cut deeply. This is the challenge I face: People often feel free to critique me. Sometimes they gossip about me. There are even people who attack me face-to-face. There are times I want to lash back, speak my mind, tell them what I really think, and in these moments my words would not be very pastoral. Yet I'm called to take the high road. O God, guard my tongue. Forgive me for harsh words spoken in anger. Teach me to use what I say to bless and never to burn. And give me the wisdom to speak the truth in love, even when it's hard to do.

Reckless words pierce like a sword, but the tongue of the wise brings healing. Truthful lips endure forever, but a lying tongue lasts only a moment.

—Proverbs 12:18–19

The wise in heart are called discerning, and pleasant words promote instruction.

—Proverbs 16:21

The tongue has the power of life and death, and those who love it will eat its fruit.

—Proverbs 18:21

An anxious heart weighs a man down, but a kind word cheers him up.

—Proverbs 12:25

I love being around Ken Korver. He has been a friend and partner in ministry for more than two decades. I respect and appreciate many qualities in Ken. But at the top of the list is his ability to bless. Every time I talk to Ken, I am reminded that God loves me and rejoices over me. Ken is always quick to give an honest word of encouragement.

Although Ken is my age and we went through seminary together, he is comfortable looking me straight in the eye and saying, "Kevin, I am so proud of you. I see God at work in you!" These words go deep into my soul and inspire me to be more faithful to God's call. Each time I'm with Ken or talk with him on the phone, I am reminded of the power of blessing. His example inspires me to use my words to build others up.

Symptoms Check
My Mouth Needs Guarding

☐ I know I should encourage other leaders in my church, but I tend to notice what they could do better or what they do wrong.

- There are people on my ministry team who need a word of blessing, and I could give it. But I'm afraid that if I'm too positive, they might start slacking off.

- I see things in others that I could bless or affirm, but being an encourager takes time and energy that I just don't have.

- Sometimes the thought goes through my mind, "No one encourages me or tells me what I am doing well; why should I spend time affirming others?"

Creating a Culture of Blessing

Churches where words of kindness and encouragement are plentiful have the aroma of life. I have walked into congregations and felt the health and joy that exist because of their culture of blessing. The opposite is also true. Congregations and staffs that are filled with criticism, backbiting, and gossip have the stench of death. Wise leaders use their words to build up others and strategically create a culture of affirmation in the church. Although we may be tempted to be critical and negative, the antidote for this behavior is learning to bless.

At Corinth Church, we have used the practice of writing notes as a way to make encouragement easy for everyone. Years ago we had an artist in the church create four different cards with our church logo and a few words on the cover: "Praying for you," "Thank you," "A note from the Pastor," and a catchall card for any other kind of note. Every staff member keeps these cards in their desk and is expected to use them often. The cards are a reminder of the value of a handwritten note of encouragement.

Occasionally at a staff meeting, we will hand out some blank "Thank You" cards or "Praying for you" cards and write notes as part of our meeting. This is a simple way to help people get (and stay) in the habit of blessing others, and over the years, a culture of encouragement has emerged. It's normal to walk into a staff member's work space and see numerous notes on the desk or posted on the wall.

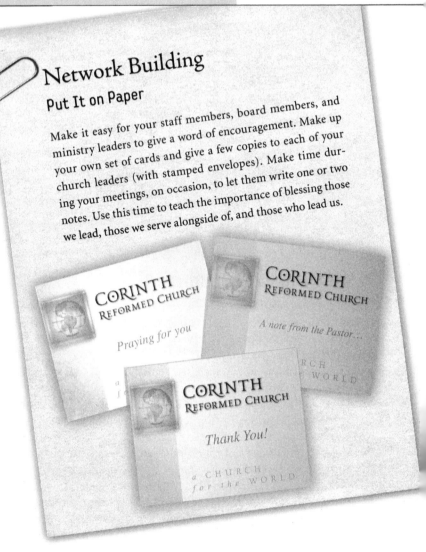

Network Building

Put It on Paper

Make it easy for your staff members, board members, and ministry leaders to give a word of encouragement. Make up your own set of cards and give a few copies to each of your church leaders (with stamped envelopes). Make time during your meetings, on occasion, to let them write one or two notes. Use this time to teach the importance of blessing those we lead, those we serve alongside of, and those who lead us.

Years ago I was convicted of the importance of encouraging others with a brief note. So on my daily work sheet, I added three items: write one note to a staff member and write two notes to church members. Six days a week, I send out three handwritten notes of blessing and encouragement. Most of these are only three or four lines, but they mean more than you can imagine.

If I sit down to write these notes and can't think of who needs a card, I just pray quietly and wait. "God, who needs a word of blessing? Who needs encouragement today? Who do you want to touch with your grace?" I wait in listening prayer until a name, situation, or face comes to mind. Once I have a sense of who needs a word of blessing, I write. It's amazing how often these people, the ones God has placed on my heart, call me or catch me at church and say, "Thank you for the note. It came at just the right time!"

One Sunday I was reminded just how important this discipline is. A volunteer on the church technical team caught me after worship. This guy looks like Jesse "the Body" Ventura (former professional wrestler and governor of Minnesota). He is a strong, self-assured man's man. With tenderness in his eyes, he said, "Pastor, I need to tell you something. Over the years, you have written me a number of notes telling me how God has used me and how much God loves me. I have kept every one of them. I keep them in a box at home. When I get discouraged and wonder if God can really do something with my life, I take out those notes and read them. I just thought you should know!"

His words surprised me. I knew the practice of writing cards was important, but the sincerity in his voice and the look in his eyes spurred me to even greater diligence and reminded me why I need to encourage other leaders to do the same.

Network Building
Over-the-Top Blessing

My wife, Sherry, was talking with a friend who attends a wonderful Assembly of God church in Grand Rapids. Her friend said with excitement, "We prayed for your church on Sunday! Every week our pastor prays for a local church and pastor during our worship service. This week he prayed for Corinth Church and Pastor Kevin Harney."

continued ↻

A couple of days later, I received a note in the mail from Pastor Sam, from Grand Rapids First Church. He wanted me to know that he prayed for our church and for me as a pastor the previous Sunday. He also wanted me to know that he would keep praying throughout the week. Little did he know that I was in a time of major ministry transition and that I needed his prayers.

This is blessing above and beyond the call of duty. Many pastors see other congregations as competition rather than as partners in ministry. Sam's example blessed me and reminded me that God's desire is for us to work together to bring God's grace to our community. I think this example should be followed by churches all over the world. What partnerships might the Holy Spirit forge and what friendships might emerge if local church leaders blessed each other with heartfelt prayers and notes of encouragement every week?

Along with written words of encouragement, good leaders know the value of blessing with our mouths. There are times when we can speak words of affirmation to the whole congregation. We can celebrate when we see God's people serving, sacrificing, and loving. It is right and good for a leader to lavish affirmation on the whole church.

We can also pick up the phone and call people who are serving faithfully. A short message on their voice mail, a text message, or a few words on the phone can lift spirits and make someone's day.

We can also get face to face, lock eyes, and speak blessing from our hearts. For some, doing this is a little uncomfortable. And it can be awkward for some to receive such a blessing. But these moments are pregnant with the presence of the Holy Spirit. Healing is unleashed through words of blessing. Friendships are forged. God shows up in these times and builds his church. We need to make face-to-face affirmation routine.

I've Got Your Back
Help Me Be One Who Blesses

Are you good at blessing and affirming others? Or are you prone to be critical? Do a mini-360 to find out how you can grow in this area of leadership. Choose three people to help you: one whom you lead, one who is a partner in ministry, and one who has a leadership or mentoring role in your life. Ask them three questions:

1. If you know of a person who has been hurt because of my words, what do you think I need to do to heal and restore this relationship?
2. What advice would you give to help me be more effective at guarding my words and becoming more encouraging of others?
3. Who are two people you feel could use a word of blessing from me?

If you want to go the next level in accountability, invite these people to give you input on these three questions any time they feel it would be helpful.

The book of Proverbs makes it clear that life and death are wrapped up in the power of our words. Healthy leaders decide to learn how to bless others frequently and freely. They also create a culture in which encouragement is normative, woven into the fabric of the church.

Creating a No-Gossip Zone

Christians have conflict with each other. Relationships get strained, communication breaks down, and tension grows. We are just people, and we face the same relational challenges anyone else does. The difference is we have crystal-clear guidelines on how to respond in these times of hurt and frustration. We are not allowed to gossip (Rom. 1:29; 2 Cor. 12:20). We can't wander around the church and vent our frustration to every person we meet. We certainly are not to speak poorly of others and dress it up as a prayer request.

Jesus has given us a simple process for dealing with relational fractures. Jesus said, "If your brother sins against you, go and show him his fault, just between the two of you. If he listens to you, you have won your brother over. But if he will not listen, take one or two others along, so that 'every matter may be established by the testimony of two or three witnesses.' If he refuses to listen to them, tell it to the church; and if he refuses to listen even to the church, treat him as you would a pagan or a tax collector" (Matt. 18:15–17).

For over a decade, the members and staff of Corinth Church have used this text as the indisputable rule for dealing with conflict. It has led to a level of unity and peace in the church that has been a joy to experience. This passage is one of the best-known, least-used portions of the Bible. So many church leaders are aware of it and believe it is true, but they don't graft it onto the church culture.

There are four basic steps to biblical conflict management. Each has guidelines for behavior as well as implications for what we cannot do in our communication. Here is how we have interpreted and applied this passage in how we do life together in the local church.

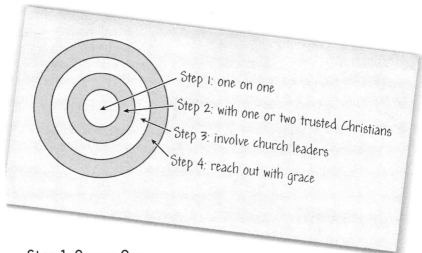

Step 1: One on One

If you have an issue with someone, you are compelled to go to this person one-on-one to work it out. This means you *can't* talk about your frustration with anyone else. You can't drop hints about it with another staff member. You can't ask for prayer in a way that subtly reveals details of the conflict, thereby gossiping. You can't let anyone else know that you have an issue with another staff member unless you have first gone to that staff member and sought to be reconciled. You also can't merely lock your frustration inside and decide to just live with your hurt and anger. Jesus makes it clear you are compelled to work the problem out.

Healthy church leaders learn how to meet with people who have sinned against them and share their heart. They seek reconciliation. They don't bury bitterness and let it poison their soul. They know that face-to-face encounters lead to restoration.

Step 2: With One or Two Trusted Christians

If you have gone to the person one-on-one and tried to work out the issue you have with them, but the two of you are not able to reconcile, you can invite one or two other trusted Christians to help in the process of healing this relationship. This doesn't mean that once you have tried to reconcile, you can now gossip and talk freely about the person who has hurt you. What it means is you can prayerfully discern who might be best to sit with the two of you the next time you meet and seek restoration in your relationship. This step is not optional. If you have sought healing in your relationship with a person on your staff or in your church, and it is not coming, you are compelled to keep working at it. The people you involve in the process are there not to gang up on the other person but to help in the process of reconciliation. At Corinth we have found that most of the relational roadblocks that can't be removed by a one-on-one conversation get resolved when wise counsel enters the process.

Step 3: Involve Church Leaders

If the inclusion of other godly people in the process doesn't lead to relational healing, bring your concern and the desire for a restoration to your church leaders. In our church tradition, this is the board of elders. For others, it could be a church board, management team, deacons, or another group. When Jesus calls us to "tell it to the church" if steps one and two have not brought the desired result, he isn't saying we can gossip about this person or announce their sin during a Sunday service. Rather, he's saying that because healthy relationships in the body of Christ are so important, you will sometimes need to bring the concern to a body of leaders who represent the wisdom of the congregation. Over more than a decade of implementing this process in the life of Corinth Church, we had only about a dozen situations that needed to enter this step in the process. I would say half of these were resolved after drawing on the counsel and wisdom of our elders board.

Step 4: Reach Out with Grace

Finally, if the person refuses any movement toward a healed relationship after steps one through three, Jesus calls us to treat the person like a "pagan or tax collector." If the leaders of the church bring their wisdom, prayers, and authority to bear on the situation and the person still refuses reconciliation, this man or woman must be treated as a sinner.

It is important to notice that Jesus is speaking to his disciples when he teaches about how we are to deal with those who have sinned against us (Matt. 18:1). The disciples have watched Jesus reach out to sinners, redeem tax collectors, restore the morally impure, and share meals with people that a normal rabbi would have avoided. They have seen Jesus love tax collectors and embrace sinners. They would have known what the Savior was getting at. Once again, his wisdom was countercultural and went against the religious norms of the day. The final step in the process is to reach out with grace and treat the person as if he or she needs to be converted.

Too often church leaders have read these words as a call to exclude people, drive them away, or cut them off from fellowship. I believe this is wrong. How did Jesus treat tax collectors and sinners? Did he exclude them? Did he hate them? Did he cast them out? No! Jesus shared meals with them, he loved them, he reached out to them with compassion and tenderness. Jesus calls the church to treat those who refuse reconciliation as if they need the love, grace, and power we can bring to their lives. We are to seek to win them to the heart of Jesus through loving and consistent prayer, service, and keeping the door open for reconciliation.

It has been amazing to see how consistently relationships have been healed by following this simple process. What is surprising is how many churches allow gossip and grumbling to exist as a cultural norm. When this happens, a poison spreads through the body. To avoid gossip, Corinth Church has implemented a number of church-wide measures.

I've Got Your Back

Take It Seriously!

Over the years, the leadership team at Corinth has continued to raise the bar on following Jesus' counsel in Matthew 18:15–17. Here are some of the ways we have done so:

continued ↪

- We address this topic in every new members class. We study the passage together and make sure that all those who join the church understand what Jesus taught. We make it clear how we operate as a church. We have actually had people decide not to join because they feel these guidelines are too strict! These have rarely been new believers but are usually long-term churchgoers coming from congregations where gossip and a complaining spirit were tolerated.
- We cover this topic in our employee handbook. All staff members know that gossip and grumbling will not be tolerated. As leaders in the church, they are expected to be models of following Jesus' teaching on this topic.
- We preach on this topic once a year and make sure the whole congregation keeps it in the front of their minds.
- We practice Christian discipline. If a person continues in the sin of gossip and spreads poison in the church, a pastor and an elder will meet with this person and call him or her to stop living contrary to Scripture.

Can you imagine a church in which there is virtually no gossip and grumbling? I can, and it is a wonderful thing!

The Blessing of Speaking the Truth in Love

We are called to use our words to bless and build up. We model healthy leadership when we create a gossip-free culture in which relationships are restored by following Jesus' teaching on reconciliation. So is there ever a time to express concerns? If we are loving toward others and never speak ill of them, how can we sharpen each other by expressing honest concerns? Is there a place for speaking the truth in love (Eph. 4:15) and sharpening those God has placed in our lives?

Leaders are called to speak the truth, but always in love. The problem comes when we err on one side or the other. When we speak the truth carelessly or harshly, our words might be true and even from the Lord, but they cut so deeply that the recipient can't hear what we say. The other extreme is when we are so tenderhearted that we refuse to speak the truth when it needs to be expressed. Wise leaders learn to resist these two temptations. Loveless truth can be damaging. Tenderness that refuses to speak the truth is equally dangerous.

Help from My Friends
How Do You Remain Accountable?

I have an accountability group of five people. Three are YFC board members and the other is a former staff worker. We meet about once a month for three hours or more. A lot of the time is spent chatting about our lives and things that are happening in Sri Lanka and in the church. We also report on our areas of weakness, which are known to the group.

Sometimes I contact the group members through a text message or phone call and report how I'm doing between meetings. When I'm traveling, I can be tempted to watch too much TV or view an unedifying program. If this happens, I send a text message to my group members so they can pray and keep me accountable. After I complete an international trip, I give them a moral report to let them know of any compromise or area of temptation I faced. I also share this report with Nelun, my wife.

— Ajith Fernando, Director, Youth for Christ, Sri Lanka

I am so thankful God has filled my life with people who, in an effort to make me more of the person God would have me to be, love me enough to speak the truth, but with tenderness. Three of the core staff members that I have served with at Corinth have the gift of a tender heart. Deb, Barb, and Ryan have always been quick to point out when I lack sensitivity or awareness of people's feelings (and this is often). They do it gently, and once I hear their words and reflect on them prayerfully, I almost always agree and follow their counsel. My wife also plays an important role in helping me see when my attitude is poor or my actions are inconsistent with what God would have me do. God uses her words, almost daily, to awaken me to areas I need to grow in. I thank God for the people in my life who speak the truth in love to me. I am a better leader because of them.

I've Got Your Back
Will You Be a Truth-Teller in My Life?

There are two parts to having your leadership life sharpened by a loving truth-teller. First, you must be willing to receive their words and thank them for daring to challenge you. If you have no one in your life that ever comes to you and speaks the hard truth, it's probably your fault. It means that you don't receive counsel well and people are afraid to share with you what God places on their hearts. They know you will shut them out or that they will pay the consequences. First, you must pray for a humble and teachable heart.

The second part is finding people with wisdom whom you trust and inviting them to speak the truth to you. It takes courage, but leaders who want to stay healthy will give a handful of people permission to play this role in their lives. If you seek out these kinds of people, they will cover your back and their counsel will spare you all kinds of heartache.

When Corinth Church decided to develop a mentoring program to invest in the lives of emerging leaders, one result was that our leaders had to learn how to speak the truth in love. When Adam Barr came to Corinth, he was an amazingly gifted leader who also happened to be an administrative nightmare. (He would be the first to say he could not administrate his way out of a paper bag.) We identified this weakness right away and spoke to him about it. Then I took him on a field trip with our other intern, Ryan. We went to Office Max and took a walk down the aisle where the planners were shelved. (This was before PDAs had come on the scene.)

I introduced Adam to the concept of keeping a detailed personal schedule of meetings, responsibilities, and important dates. We talked about planning. I came up with two mantras that I've used many times since then as we've mentored emerging leaders. The first one is, "Anyone can own a date book (PDA), but a leader knows how to use it." The second is, "In ministry, every detail has a name attached to it. When you forget a detail, you forget a person."

One aspect of the church's intern ministry is to identify areas of weakness and examine them. This can't happen if being nice trumps speaking the truth. There simply are times when a leader needs to look at a person and say, "You have a weakness here. You need to change; you need to grow. You are in danger of hurting the church if you don't grow up." This should be done with kindness and sensitivity, but it must be done!

One of the greatest joys in my ministry was when I got a report from Adam about six months after he had left Corinth Church. He was on staff at a church in the Chicago area and was having a great time in ministry. During a conversation, he said to me, "The office manager at the church actually thinks I'm an administrative god!" We both laughed, very hard. I said, "Are you serious?" He assured me that she was amazed by the way he planned, never missed details, and always got things in to her on time. She loved him.

What a glorious reminder of the value of speaking the truth in love. Although the process was difficult and it was hard for Adam to face an area of weakness, he has made this an area of strength. It would have been wrong to protect his feelings by neglecting this area for the sake of being kind. And Adam would be the first to tell you that he is truly thankful that someone loved him enough to point out an area he needed to grow in, loved him along the way, and helped him take steps toward becoming the leader God wants him to be.

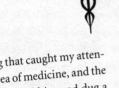

Doctor's Insight

Don't Tell Me the Truth!

As I sat with Dr. Baxter, he said something that caught my attention. We were conversing about his specific area of medicine, and the line that struck me was just an aside, but I stopped him and dug a little deeper. He had commented, "Sometimes when I give a diagnosis that a patient does not want to hear, they get angry at me."

I probed, "Do they stay angry, or do they get over it pretty quickly?"

He responded, "Most who get angry come to realize that I am trying to help, but some actually blame me for the diagnosis. They see their condition as my fault."

I pushed again, "Do any of these patients leave and refuse treatment?"

His response surprised me but was consistent with what I've seen in ministry when people speak the truth to each other. He said, "I have patients who are so angry at me because of the diagnosis that they don't come back. They refuse to hear the truth. They won't own their part in their condition."

I asked a final question and was saddened by Dr. Baxter's answer. "Do these people find another doctor and get the help they need?"

He said, "Some do, but I have had patients who refuse to face the truth. They don't come back to me, and they won't go see another doctor. They choose to live with the consequences rather than get the help they need."

I could see the sadness in his eyes. He cares and wants to help these people. But he knows that he can't force them to accept the truth.

Truth-Telling and Church Discipline

There was a day when people spoke of the "marks of the true church." It may not be in vogue today, but back when people spoke of it, they listed items such as preaching the Word of God, administration of the sacraments, and the practice of church discipline, to name a few. For centuries, the church emphasized disciplining members who indulged in unrepented sin, damaging their lives and walk with Christ. Sadly, in many places the practice of church discipline has gone the way of stained-glass windows, choir robes, and Sunday evening services. The few churches that practice church discipline today are vestiges of a day gone by.

Leaders and churches that are committed to speaking the truth in love learn that church discipline is part of the package. If we truly care about people, we will not look the other way while they shipwreck their faith, destroy their lives, and run from God. With tenderness and strength, we will invite them back to God's will for their lives. Discipline is not a hammer for crushing the wayward brother or sister. It's a redemptive intervention that calls people to turn back to the Lord, who loves them.

The leadership team at Corinth Church is committed to speaking the truth in love, even when it hurts. This means we practice church discipline as part of our ministry. Along the way, we have learned that the process is hard both for those who are disciplined and for us as leaders. But the healing, redemption, and wholeness that come from loving discipline have been joys to witness. It's worth the pain to see the Holy Spirit transform hearts and lives.

The staff and church board members have had to make some hard calls over the years. We have sat with people considering a divorce and studied God's Word together as we called them to hang in there and not give up on the covenant relationship they entered. We have confronted people living in sexual sin and challenged them to stop living and sleeping together until they are married. We have confronted people who are habitual gossips and taught them about God's desire for them to guard their words. We have lovingly addressed many areas of sin in an effort to help people live in a way that brings joy to God's heart.

In the process of administering discipline, we are reminded, every time, that we are broken and sinful people. Every member of our pastoral team and every elder is a forgiven sinner. We are still walking on wobbly legs, and each of us needs God's grace every day. We do not discipline as moral authorities or executioners. We come to people in their brokenness and acknowledge that we too walk by grace, and grace alone.

What we have learned is that most people appreciate and accept discipline when it is extended in love and humility. Yes, there are those who get angry or defensive or who refuse to meet with our church leaders. But most people are willing to meet and talk. We gather with one elder, one pastor, and the person who is struggling. We pray, share the concern, study the Word of God on the topic at hand, and call the person to conform to the teaching of Scripture. At that point, it's up to them. But to our amazement and delight, many of these encounters end with the person agreeing with God's Word and choosing to change the way they are living. I could fill the rest of this book with accounts of how people have experienced God's grace in these encounters, but I will close this chapter with only one story.

Dan had been attending Corinth for a few months, always sitting in the balcony and leaving during the final song. It was clear that he was in avoidance mode. When he and I finally had a chance to sit and talk, I could see the pain in his eyes. Dan was hurt; he was angry. He asked if he would be loved and accepted at our church. He wanted to know if he could join the church and not worry about his past following him.

I asked Dan to tell me his story. I wanted to know what had happened that made him feel driven out of his last church. After he told me the story, he asked, "Do you think I could join Corinth Church?" I looked at him and said, "No!" He looked very surprised. I assured him that he was welcome to come to services and that people would treat him kindly, but there was no way our board of elders would allow him to join.

You see, Dan had been an elder at his previous church. When he was ordained, he committed to live under the discipline and leadership of the church. Along the way, he had gotten involved with a woman and had an affair. The leadership team of his previous church had asked to meet with him, but he refused.

Dan looked at me and said, "I have grown to love Corinth Church. I really want to connect here. I know I have problems, and I think I can sort them out here. Is there any way I can join the church?"

I said, "Yes."

Dan paused, swallowed hard, and asked me what he had to do.

I said, "You need to go back to your church, sit with the people God has placed as spiritual leaders in your life, and listen to them. You need to be restored to those brothers and sisters."

He looked at me in stunned amazement and said, "You're serious, aren't you."

I said, "Dead serious."

Dan said, "I'll do it."

I wasn't sure I would ever see Dan again, but he showed up the next Sunday for worship. The next week, I received a call from Dan's pastor. He asked me what I had said to him. I told the pastor about our church's commitment to loving Christian discipline and that I knew there was no way our elders board would receive Dan into membership until he had accepted the discipline of his church. He told me that Dan had called and he was going to meet with their elders. I promised to pray for the meeting, and we hung up.

About a week later, the pastor of Dan's church called me again. I asked him how the meeting went. He said, "It was one of our best elders meetings ever! There was repentance, restoration, and healing. Tears were shed, and the Holy Spirit showed up." I rejoiced with him and he thanked our leaders for having the courage to love Dan enough to speak the truth and help them practice loving discipline. He told me that his board was amazed that another church would take discipline so seriously. He let me know that they were encouraged to be more diligent in this area of ministry. My prayer is that this story will inspire other leaders and churches to discover the healing potential of spiritual discipline.

Self-Examination Suggestion
Speaking the Truth in Loving Discipline

Most church leaders know that discipline is essential for a church to be healthy. If a leader or board refuses to practice loving discipline, the cost will be high. Yet many churches look the other way as church members spiral downward in sinful patterns that are never addressed by their leadership.

Take a moment to reflect on the following questions:

1. Do the leaders of your church practice church discipline? If yes, do you exercise it with humble hearts and a vision to transform lives?

2. If your church leaders do not exercise consistent and loving discipline, why is this key element missing?

3. What can you do as a leader to help your church embrace the goodness of Christian discipline?

Humble Service Reveals Jesus' Presence

The Leader's Hands

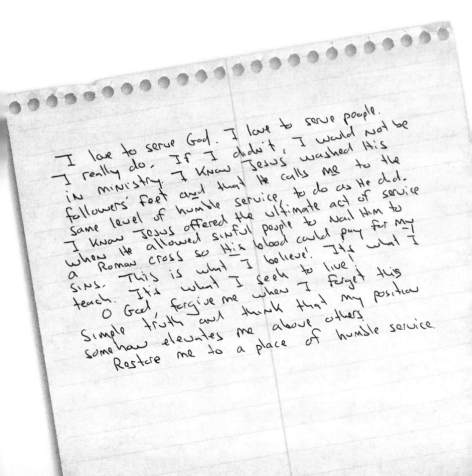

I love to serve God. I love to serve people. I really do. If I didn't, I would not be in ministry. I know Jesus washed His followers' feet and that He calls me to the same level of humble service, to do as He did. I know Jesus offered the ultimate act of service when He allowed sinful people to nail Him to a Roman cross so His blood could pay for my sins. This is what I believe. It's what I teach. It's what I seek to live!

O God, forgive me when I forget this simple truth and think that my position somehow elevates me above others. Restore me to a place of humble service.

> In the same way, you who are younger, submit your-
> selves to your elders. All of you, clothe yourselves with
> humility toward one another, because, "God opposes the
> proud but shows favor to the humble and oppressed."
> Humble yourselves, therefore, under God's mighty
> hand, that he may lift you up in due time.
>
> —1 Peter 5:5–6 (TNIV)

> "You call me 'Teacher' and 'Lord,' and rightly so, for that
> is what I am. Now that I, your Lord and Teacher, have
> washed your feet, you also should wash one another's
> feet."
>
> —John 13:13–14

It was Easter Sunday, and the congregation had gathered to celebrate Jesus' resurrection. Everyone was dressed in their best church
clothes, and there was excitement in the air. Like every Easter, there
was a buzz of joy and anticipation, a sense that the risen Christ would
bless each person gathered with a profound sense of his presence.

Then, completely unannounced, he showed up.

A man with long brown hair and a flowing robe walked down the
center aisle of the church, his arms stretched out as if to embrace the
whole congregation. He declared to all those gathered that he was
Jesus.

A hush fell over the worship center. The lead pastor, who was
standing in the pulpit, swallowed hard, prayed, and tried to shape
the right response to this surprise visitor. With great wisdom, the
pastor said to the would-be-Jesus, "Show me the scars on your hands
where you were nailed to the cross."

An awkward silence hung in the air. Then the robed man spoke,
"I had them removed."

The pastor declared, "Jesus would never have his scars removed."
And he asked the ushers to help the confused man out of the
church.

I was not there that Easter morning, but I heard the pastor who
faced this unique challenge tell this story. I think his response to the
surprise visitor was inspired. He asked to see the scars on his hands,

reminders of Jesus' ultimate act of service. When it became clear there were no scars, the pastor knew it could not be Jesus.

Those who follow the crucified and risen Savior are called to offer humble service in the name of the one who bore the nails for them. Those who are going to lead learn quickly that serving is foundational to our calling. To lead like Jesus is to offer our hands to take up the cross daily, to pick up the towel and the basin, to serve as he did.

Sadly, many in Christian ministry have forgotten the service part of the equation. As people in our congregations put us on a pedestal, we can begin to feel a bit exalted. As a church grows, it's all too easy to believe that certain tasks are simply below our station. We prefer a manicure to having calloused hands.

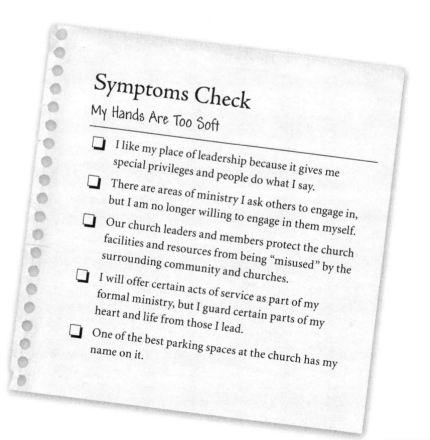

Symptoms Check
My Hands Are Too Soft

- ❏ I like my place of leadership because it gives me special privileges and people do what I say.
- ❏ There are areas of ministry I ask others to engage in, but I am no longer willing to engage in them myself.
- ❏ Our church leaders and members protect the church facilities and resources from being "misused" by the surrounding community and churches.
- ❏ I will offer certain acts of service as part of my formal ministry, but I guard certain parts of my heart and life from those I lead.
- ❏ One of the best parking spaces at the church has my name on it.

Getting Your Hands Dirty

In the time when Jesus walked through the Middle East, the custom of washing feet was common. When travelers came in from the dusty roads, there was often a bowl of water and a towel near the door. Household servants would render this simple and humble service—washing people's dirty feet. But if there was no servant present, the host (or the first guest to arrive) would often take this responsibility.

As Jesus and his followers gathered for what would become known as the Last Supper (John 13:1–17), there was no servant present to wash feet. One by one the disciples walked past the bowl and towel sitting in plain view. The same men who had watched Jesus model humble service countless times refused to wash each others' feet or the feet of Jesus. No one got their hands dirty.

They all sat down with hot, sweaty, smelly feet covered with dust. In the middle of the meal, Jesus got up from the table, took the bowl and towel, and washed their feet. The divine hands that had shaped the heavens and earth now scrubbed the filthy feet of human beings. The hands that sustain the universe gently dried their calloused feet. He even washed Judas's feet, though he knew that Judas would soon betray him. After this shocking act of service, Jesus said, "You call me 'Teacher' and 'Lord,' and rightly so, for that is what I am. Now that I, your Lord and Teacher, have washed your feet, you also should wash one another's feet. I have set you an example that you should do as I have done for you. I tell you the truth, no servant is greater than his master, nor is a messenger greater than the one who sent him. Now that you know these things, you will be blessed if you do them" (John 13:13–17).

This call, to a band of fresh new leaders who would soon guide the church into its infancy, was clear. It rings through time and speaks to leaders today. The way of Jesus is the way of humble service. The hands that washed the disciples' feet would soon be nailed to a cross. This ultimate act of service and love cost Jesus his life. Our Lord was willing to get his hands dirty and bloody to show us what a true leader looks like.

Self-Examination Suggestion
Hand Exam

Look at your hands. Are they the hands of a servant? Are they dirty from washing feet? Are they bloodstained from taking up the cross daily and following Jesus? Take some time for reflection and ask yourself:

- Do I serve freely and joyfully?
- Do I regularly serve the people in my congregation?
- Am I known in my neighborhood and community as one who serves others?

During my first board meeting at Corinth Church, I looked slowly around the room and studied the faces of the gathered leaders. There was wisdom in their eyes and love for Jesus in their hearts. Then I looked at their hands. I'm not sure why, but my eyes were drawn to their hands, and one by one, being careful that no one would notice, I studied them.

Corinth was a small country church back then. Close to half the congregation was made up of three extended families. These people were salt of the earth, hardworking and hearty. Their hands told a story. A number of the men were missing all or part of a finger. All had calluses that revealed a lifetime of long days in the fields, in the workshop, or doing some kind of hard labor. Some hands were stained and the creases in the skin were filled with oil or material that did not wash off easily. These were leaders who knew what a hard day of physically demanding labor is like.

In the years that followed, these leaders taught me what serving looks like. They came to meetings or classes after a ten- to twelve-hour day of work. They came joyfully and ready to serve. When there was an opportunity to help someone in need or to work around the church grounds, they were ready to get their gnarled and dirty hands even dirtier.

Healthy leaders understand that washing feet leads to dirty hands. When our hands take up Jesus' cross, we get splinters, we bleed, and sometimes our hands are pierced. Hands that serve tirelessly can become calloused from the hard work of ministry.

The Danger of Delegation

In some leadership circles, the buzzword is *delegation*. As a church grows, some leaders specialize to the point they no longer do certain ministries. There is definitely a need for strategic delegation, but we can take it too far. We must always be ready to serve no matter how big our churches grow or how specialized we become in our ministries. The staff at Corinth Church will tell you that I have a gift for administration and delegation. I hope they would also tell you that there is no job or act of service that's beneath me or anyone else on the staff. Although each staff member has a detailed job description, all are expected to step in and help whenever needed, no matter how humble the act of service.

Hands ready to serve are born of a heart that loves people. I have lost track of the number of times I've seen ministry leaders at Corinth offer to help other leaders and ministries. Most of the staff specializes in a specific area, but everyone has the sense that they are also generalists.

I have watched the chair of the executive committee freely help stack chairs after a Sunday school class. I have seen the office manager, who has a rigorous schedule, go out front and water plants that need a little tender loving care. With admiration I have seen the church worship director bake snacks for church shut-ins and deliver them every Christmas. Again and again, the youth director sacrificed "their space" in the youth center because another ministry had a need. I have watched the pastor of global outreach go with a refugee family to help them learn to shop for groceries. I could fill pages with examples of leaders freely and joyfully helping others with humble acts of service. Delegation and clear ministry responsibilities are valuable. But leaders must always remember the call to serve.

Help from My Friends
How Do You Make Wise Decisions?

I listen to the question, problem, or dilemma first. Then I weigh it against Scripture. Next, I pray, either in my mind or out loud in the middle of the meeting. If I don't follow this method, I usually respond with my feelings and thoughts, both of which have one problem — me. I also have a support team, which includes my wife, Laurie, and three couples from the church. This group loves God and cares deeply about me and my family. We meet as needed to discuss my schedule, outside speaking invitations, dreams, hopes, and ideas. Very helpful!

— Bob Bouwer, Senior Pastor, Faith Church, Dyer, IN

Generous Hands

Our hope for eternity began with God's decision to give. "God so loved the world that he gave ..." (John 3:16). If we want to have hands like Jesus' hands, we need to learn generosity. Leaders are most effective when they are ready to give things away. God honors hands that are open and willing to share.

I was a sophomore in high school when I first met a Christian leader who modeled the serving hands of Jesus. Doug Drainville was a volunteer leader of the youth group at Garden Grove Community Church, which I had started attending. He became a powerful influence on my becoming a pastor who believes that serving is at the core of ministry.

I did not yet have a car or license, and Doug had a very cool VW Bug. He let me know that if I ever needed a ride somewhere, he would be glad to help. He lived about twenty minutes from my house. I am embarrassed to recall my self-centered attitude as a young believer.

I would actually call Doug on occasion to see if he could drive me to my girlfriend's house. When he was available, he always helped out. He would drive twenty minutes to my house, transport me fifteen minutes to my girlfriend's house, and drive home. He was always glad to help me. He used his gas and about an hour of his day just to serve me. When I think back, I realize that I never offered him money for gas and that there were even times I failed to thank him.

Doug's generous and senseless service has marked my life. Almost three decades later, I know that I saw Jesus in Doug's service as much as I did in any worship service in those early years of my faith. I am so grateful God placed a leader in my life who was willing to get his hands dirty. I hope my life reflects that same Christlike spirit in the way I serve others.

Network Building

An A-WICS Attitude

When Debi Rose became my ministry assistant, I learned new lessons about service. She was already our worship director. When it became clear that I needed some administrative support because the church was growing rapidly, she offered to help. With time, we formalized her role, but initially she just kept seeing where she could serve and jumped in.

Over time, I noticed that Debi would say "any way I can serve" quite a bit. If there was a need, she was quick to volunteer with a joyful heart. After I heard her response about a hundred times, I came up with an acronym, A-WICS. Since then our whole staff has adopted the phrase "an A-WICS attitude" to describe a servant's heart. Now when we interview a prospective staff member, we ask them if they are ready to come with an "any way I can serve" attitude.

If you want to build a culture of service in your church and ministry, train your leaders to adopt an A-WICS attitude.

At Corinth Church, we decided to do our best to share with our community and the church at large everything God gives us. An A-WICS attitude has spilled from our church staff to the congregation, from our congregation to our community, and from there, all over the world. As the church has grown in generosity, God has continued to entrust greater resources to our care so we can give away even more.

If Corinth has a ministry idea that is working, we tell other churches about it. When other churches or pastors ask for help, we do all we can to give what we have away. If we have resources that other churches can use, they are welcome to them. If our community has a need, we seek to meet it. Living out this passion to keep our hands open has taken on many forms. Here is a small sample:

- Over the years, some of the artists in the church have made beautiful banners for use in our worship center at different times during the year. Other churches in our community are welcome to borrow these banners, and they do.
- Every year, we hold a huge vacation Bible school program. We have a team that builds amazing sets. There are churches in our community that plan their VBS programs after ours so they can use all we have made. Then they pass these things to another church the way a family with five boys passes along blue jeans with reinforced knees. By the time the props and sets have done the local circuit, they are shot, and we are happy that they are.
- A public high school asked if they could use our church facility to hold their standardized testing for hundreds of kids. Not only did we say yes but we offered the space at no charge and offered to provide snacks. We also opened up the high school center for break times so the students could play pool, foosball, and video games as well as watch cool sports videos. Talk about building bridges with our schools!
- Corinth has developed numerous creative outreach ideas over the years, and we make a brochure explaining how church members can participate in these opportunities. Debi Rose, my ministry assistant, has sent out electronic

files of our brochures and evangelism strategies to hundreds of churches over the years. If our resources will help other congregations fulfill the Great Commission, we give them to anyone who can use them.

- For many years Corinth Church, in partnership with Faith Church in Dyer, Indiana, held a leaders gathering and brought in gifted communicators like Ben Patterson, Jerry Sitzer, Juan Carlos Ortiz, Charles Van Engen, and others to spend three days investing in a small group of pastors. If the leaders could not afford the event, church members from Corinth and Faith covered the cost. This became an intimate gathering of twenty-five to sixty leaders who needed refreshment and encouragement. It was a gift from our churches to leaders from around the United States and Canada.

- The church has also made it a practice to plan a lunch for local pastors each time we bring in a special speaker. Corinth underwrites the lunch and invites leaders from an array of denominational backgrounds to come for free, just to bless them.

- The office team at Corinth has spent thousands of dollars over the years sending books, resources, and ministry helps to other churches in the United States and around the world. The deacons approve these funds and see them as part of our congregation's ministry to the church at large. The deacons also set aside a fund to help our pastors with expenses they incur when ministering to groups that can't afford to cover travel and resource costs.

- Corinth has held many training days on topics as diverse as evangelism, leadership, and teaching children and youth about human sexuality. Each time we have a training day, we invite churches all over the greater Grand Rapids area. Years ago we had staff groups come from other churches for half a day, and our team would invest in them. When we did this, we never asked for payment for the training. Then we began offering annual formal training so we could pour into multiple churches each time and be better stewards of our staff members' energy and time.

These are just some of the ways God has led Corinth Church to live with open and generous hands. I am convinced that the commitment to sacrificial serving begins in the hearts of the church leaders and then permeates the congregation. Some years ago, Corinth adopted a slogan that now appears on our stationery, cards, and other church materials. It is simply "Corinth Reformed Church ... A Church for the World."

Network Building
Who Can We Serve?

It's a simple but culture-shifting question. What do we have that we can give away? Meet with your church leadership team and address this question. Read out loud some of the examples in this chapter, and then begin to dream. List ways your church can share facilities, resources, and ministry ideas with other congregations and your community. You will be amazed at how much you have that you can share.

Hands That Give Everything

Over the years, I have watched as the congregation at Corinth Church opened their hands and shared freely with our community and other ministries. There was a price tag every step of the way, but we pressed on. There came a point when we realized we had something else to give, something a little more complex than sharing our facilities or ministry ideas. The Holy Spirit put on the hearts of our church leaders that we needed to invest our lives in emerging leaders. We needed to give ourselves away. This led to a proposal we brought to the congregation to begin a mentoring program in which our pastors and key leaders would invest in the lives of seminary students.

A small group of people saw this as a way to get cheap help from the local seminary. They were familiar with an old model in which churches would call a seminary and ask for a pastor-in-training to help the church. When this unsuspecting victim showed up, they would throw him into a room with a bunch of junior high students and a box of curriculum. Or they would heap on the intern as much work as he could handle while paying him the lowest possible amount. The goal was to get as much out of the seminary student as possible, while investing minimal time, money, and resources.

Our vision was radically different. We wanted to pour into the lives of emerging leaders and ultimately invest in the kingdom by growing gifted and passionate pastors. We had to fight off those who were clinging to the "what can we get" model and invite the congregation to adopt a "what can we give" attitude. At the information meeting, people kept asking questions about what our church would get out of this financial investment. Would it take some of the load off of the pastors? Would it free our schedule to do other things? We had to explain that launching this new ministry would cost the church financially and that it would tax our pastors and leaders because we would be investing our lives in these future church leaders.

Our goal was to support these students so they could focus on their studies and integrate their learning in the church. This meant we were ready to help with housing, seminary costs, living expenses, cars, and whatever else was needed. As the vision became clearer, the resources came in. We set up a fellowship grant, and each intern received what was needed. There was no hourly pay or keeping of time cards. Each was supported according to their needs. This meant some interns received more than others, but all had their needs met.

The pastors and volunteer leaders began investing their lives in and nurturing our first two interns. As we did, I thought often of the apostle Paul's words, "But we were gentle among you, like a mother caring for her little children. We loved you so much that we were delighted to share with you not only the gospel of God but our lives as well, because you had become so dear to us" (1 Thess. 2:7–8).

Over the years, God led our church to pour into a number of young men. It was just as we had anticipated. The process meant a substantial investment of time as we invited each one into our lives and hearts. We helped them take all they were learning in their classes and discover what worked in the church and what needed to be left behind. These young men became part of our families as we shared life together. It was giving in a whole new way; we were giving our lives.

As I look back almost a decade later, I am thrilled with what God has done through the open hands and hearts of the people at Corinth Church. Since we began the program, we have always had at least one intern and up to four being trained at a time. From the start, we determined that we were going to avoid short-term commitments and look for emerging leaders who could be with us for three to four years. Although we thought we knew what we were getting into at the beginning, it was a greater investment than any of us ever dreamed, and it was worth every dollar and hour.

Doctor's Insight
How Can I Serve You?

Dr. John Albrecht has been our family dentist for almost two decades. I met him when I moved to Grand Rapids and attended my first board meeting at Zion Church. John was an elder and the clerk of the board, and I had the privilege of being one of his pastors for a number of years. I was immediately struck by his gentle spirit and wise insight during our meetings.

Eighteen years later, I sat with John in the living room of his home and had a fascinating conversation. One theme that came up over and over was the importance of listening as we serve people. When John begins with a new patient, he asks questions such as:

continued ⇨

- On a scale of one to ten, how healthy is your mouth?
- On a scale of one to ten, how healthy do you want your mouth to be?

Then, he listens. He asks a battery of questions and soaks in the responses of his patients. Some feel free to respond, and others resist, but in every case, John listens. He says that this process at the start of a relationship with a new patient is critical for him as a doctor. Then as the years pass, he continues to ask questions and listen. He also has trained his staff to ask probing questions and listen closely to patients' responses.

What Dr. Albrecht has learned, and taught me, is that listening precedes serving. He knows how to help his patients because he has taken the time to hear them. Their insights, perspectives, and diagnoses help shape the direction he will go in their treatment. As leaders who want to serve people at their point of need, we become more effective when we ask good questions and listen attentively. What we hear will shape our service.

Every one of the interns trained at Corinth is engaged in fruitful and Christ-honoring ministry. Adam Barr has started a ministry called Borderlands that helps build bridges for high school students as they get ready to enter the world of college. This worldview ministry is touching many students and churches. Ryan is on the core staff at Corinth Church and is leading the adult spiritual formation ministry. Mark is a missionary in the Muslim world, bringing the gospel to one of the most challenging places on the face of the earth. Jag is a chaplain working in New Jersey with adults who have special needs. (Just as a fun little sidenote, all four of these interns married women named Jen.) Cody is a pastor at a church in the Minneapolis area. Travis is still in seminary and is presently being mentored at the church and leading the ministry to young adults. Corinth's commitment to invest, life on life, in future leaders will bear kingdom fruit that we will see only on the other side of eternity.

As the hands of the people at Corinth have become more and more open, the church's influence has grown. God has pressed us to share our finances, our facilities, and our ministry ideas. But beyond all of this, he has called us to share our lives, our homes, our families, and our very hearts. As we have done this, new leaders have been raised up and the church has been strengthened.

chapter 7

Laughter Sustains

Our Sanity

The Leader's Funny Bone

I need to laugh more than I do. I sat with a woman whose husband, the man who said, "for better and for worse," ran off with a woman half his age. I cared, prayed, and felt helpless to relieve her deep pain. I battled through a board meeting with a gifted group of leaders who couldn't resolve a critical issue. I did a funeral for a seven-year-old boy whose body had been ravaged by leukemia. I processed ministry challenges with a volunteer who does not really fit where she is serving. Have you ever had to fire a volunteer? As the week comes to a close, I could really use a friend who will talk with me, laugh with me, go see a comedy with me. Sometimes I feel that if I can't laugh, I'll lose my mind. And, some days laughter is hard to come by.

A happy heart makes the face cheerful, but heartache crushes the spirit.... All the days of the oppressed are wretched, but the cheerful heart has a continual feast.

—Proverbs 15:13, 15

Nehemiah said, "Go and enjoy choice food and sweet drinks, and send some to those who have nothing prepared. This day is sacred to our Lord. Do not grieve, for the joy of the LORD is your strength."

—Nehemiah 8:10

Our mouths were filled with laughter, our tongues with songs of joy. Then it was said among the nations, "The LORD has done great things for them."

—Psalm 126:2

Have you ever watched two dogs meet for the first time? There's a lot of posturing, sometimes fighting, and often a ritual of butt sniffing. They growl and size each other up in their own canine way. This kind of behavior is not reserved only for poodles and pit bulls; it's also often the behavior of pastors.

When I showed up at the Glen Eyrie conference center in Colorado Springs, testosterone was already in the air. The event was designed to bring together young pastors who were leading growing churches. These congregations were identified as "islands of health and strength." I'm still not exactly sure what an island of health and strength looks like or why I was invited, but I went anyway. Hey, free trip to Colorado ... what can I say? There were just over twenty leaders present, all were men, and the sense of competition was palpable.

In the wild, gorillas and other primates pound their chests and grunt at each other, and rams butt heads to establish dominance. It's a sad reality that when pastors get together, there's often lots of chest thumping too. Of course, we were more refined and subtle than wild animals. We didn't literally butt heads or thump our chests. What we did that first evening of the Leadership Network Young Leaders Gathering was power up with comments about the size of our churches, budgets, and acreage. We played the "mine is bigger than yours" game.

I watched the drama unfold over that first day. I was the only one there mature enough to stay out of all the silly posturing ... I wish. The truth is, I acted as immaturely as the rest of the group. The goal of the event was to create time for "cutting edge" leaders to converse about what was effective and bearing fruit in their ministries. The staff of Leadership Network was there to listen, observe, and learn. They would chronicle the stories and lessons, compile them, and share their learning with the church at large.

I'm pretty sure the facilitators saw right away what was happening. By the first evening, the leader of the event suggested we depart from the agenda and just tell stories. The invitation was simple; tell a story about a time you did something in ministry that tanked, bombed, or spun out of control.

This little exercise was the catalyst for the rest of our time together.

Over the next few hours, we let down our guard. We stopped thumping our chests and began laughing. We laughed at ourselves and with each other. It was healing, cathartic, grace-filled. One pastor shared about an Easter service he led in a casino and how a man came forward to receive Jesus wearing a giant, pink bunny rabbit suit. His contract with the casino kept him from taking off the giant bunny head while in public. As he came forward, he was sobbing, and the huge pink ears bobbed uncontrollably. This story opened the floodgate, releasing accounts of hilarious ministry moments, painfully funny lapses in judgment, and stories of incompetence that demanded a full measure of God's grace.

Something mysterious, sacred, and holy happened as we shared our stories. We laughed so hard our sides hurt and we could hardly breathe. Tears of joy flowed. The Holy Spirit appeared, and we were no longer dynamic young leaders; we were children.

At that point, almost all of the posturing ended, and we began communicating in a different way—with vulnerability and honesty. Dare I say there were moments of authentic humility? I am deeply thankful for that gathering because a number of those men have become lifelong friends and partners in ministry.

There's something powerful about laughter. When we laugh with others, we take ourselves a little less seriously. I am convinced that in times of joy-filled laughter, we see Jesus' face, and the kingdom of God comes near.

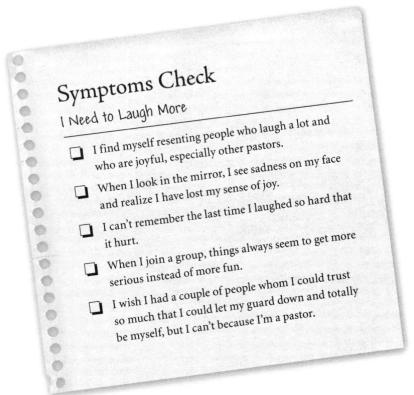

Symptoms Check

I Need to Laugh More

☐ I find myself resenting people who laugh a lot and who are joyful, especially other pastors.

☐ When I look in the mirror, I see sadness on my face and realize I have lost my sense of joy.

☐ I can't remember the last time I laughed so hard that it hurt.

☐ When I join a group, things always seem to get more serious instead of more fun.

☐ I wish I had a couple of people whom I could trust so much that I could let my guard down and totally be myself, but I can't because I'm a pastor.

Discover the Power of Joy-Filled Laughter

I have met leaders who know how to laugh. I have also encountered pastors who seem to be unfamiliar with sidesplitting humor. I find that I more quickly trust those who can laugh than those who struggle to crack a smile. There is power and health in laughter. At Corinth we have learned to affirm play, encourage joy, and create opportunities for laughter. We experience God's grace in these moments, and through them we grow closer to each other and to Jesus. Let me make it very clear that the leaders at Corinth Church work with intense diligence. We are serious when the moment demands it. We are compassionate, and we have shed many tears of sorrow together. But we are also an absolute hoot and know how to crack each other up.

An epic moment of laughter that we often recount began as I sat at my desk one fall afternoon. The phone rang. It was Barb, our office manager. She informed me that Emily from Bronner's Christmas Wonderland, the world's largest Christmas store, was on the phone and wanted to talk with me about our church doing a "living nativity" for Christmas. There had been some buzz among a few people who were enthused about putting on a nativity scene with live animals, so I had an idea where this was coming from. I reminded Barb that the church board had decided this wasn't the year for such an "extravaganza." I asked her to tell Emily we would not be putting on a living nativity this year, but thanks for calling.

A few minutes later, my phone rang again. It was Barb. Apparently Emily had persuaded her to ask me if I would give her just a few minutes. Emily was sure that she could help me see the value of doing a living nativity. I assured Barb I was not going to engage in a conversation with Emily and asked her to explain this to the persistent Christmas specialist.

About five minutes later, my phone rang and Barb informed me that my sister was on the phone with an emergency. I quickly hit the flashing line to see which of my three sisters was calling with a crisis.

"Pastor Harney, please don't be angry. This is Emily from Bronner's Christmas store, and I am soooo excited about helping your church do a living nativity. If you'll give me just a few minutes of your time, I'm sure you will see the value of this program. We would be thrilled if you would let us bring the sights, sounds, and smells of the first Christmas into your worship center."

I was speechless. I sat there listening to her sales pitch because I didn't know what to say. She hurried through her script and at the very end informed me that if I acted right away, we could reserve Gus the Grunting Camel for our living nativity. According to Emily, this highly gifted camel would kneel next to the baby Jesus and grunt out a recognizable version of "Silent Night."

I told Emily to hold for a moment and rang the front office. Barb answered and I asked her if the woman on the phone had actually called the office and claimed to be my sister with an emergency. Barb said she had.

I picked up the line and explained to Emily how I felt about her pretending she was calling about a family emergency. She responded, "It would be an emergency if you missed these great prices." I let her know, in no uncertain terms, that we would not be doing a living nativity with her, this year or ever.

A short time later, my phone rang again. It was Barb calling to inform me that I had been, depending on your generation, on *Candid Camera*, punk'd, X'd. The entire encounter had been staged. We had recently brought in a pastor to be trained to lead a church that our congregation was planting. Josh Blunt, who now leads our daughter church, Wayfarer Community Church, had formulated the plan, written the script, and talked his wife, Jaime, into calling and harassing me.

This was the start of a series of very fun and funny interactions with Josh over the years. Our staff loves to laugh and occasionally plays pranks on each other. Josh and Jaime fit right in, and their bold plan to mess with me was immediately embraced by the rest of the staff.

After the Gus the Grunting Camel episode, one of the pastors, Don Porter, suggested we do something to get Josh back. I assured him we would. But I said we should wait for the right opportunity. Immediate retaliation is predictable and boring. What we needed was patience and attentiveness. I am a firm believer that God always provides.

As time passed, the perfect moment fell right into our laps. It was late one snowy winter night, and Josh made a mistake he would never forget. But that story will have to wait.

Self-Examination Suggestion

Ask yourself these questions and answer honestly:

1. When people are with me, do they usually leave with a smile on their face?

2. Do I laugh often, and do others laugh with me?

3. Do I create experiences and moments of play, fun, and laughter for the people I am called to lead?

Create Space to Laugh, Play, and Have Fun

Of all the people on the face of the earth, Christians should be the most joyful.

Of all the places in the world, the church should overflow most freely with joy and laughter.

Do you agree with these statements? I do! I believe leaders can take themselves too seriously. And if we aren't careful, we can force everyone else to take us too seriously. There are moments for sobriety, somberness, and quiet reverence, and these will come often in ministry. But healthy leaders know there needs to be balance.

I can't recall a single staff meeting when we did not laugh. I really can't. We always have an agenda and we cover key issues, pray together, and report on needs in our areas of ministry. But the first fifteen minutes always seem to lead to some kind of laughter. There are times when we laugh so hard it hurts and tears flow.

There have been meetings when someone played a clip from a TV show such as *The King of Queens* or *The Office*. Sometimes Debi Rose gives an update on one of her pets that ends up being hilarious. Maybe Don Porter tells a story (usually we have heard it a dozen times) with no particular point except to crack us up. It's rarely planned, but we laugh. I think what helps is that we make space for play, for natural interaction, for life. Our agenda guides us, but it's not a taskmaster. When staff meetings follow an exclusively corporate model, we lose life-giving moments of human interaction.

Network Building
Planning Play

As a leader, you have a unique opportunity. You can set the agenda and actually plan to have fun. Look at the agenda for your next staff meeting or your next leadership team meeting. Then get creative. Figure out ways to make time for fun, play, and even laughter with your ministry team. Just to get the juices flowing, here are some of the things we have done:

continued ⇨

- One sunny day, we borrowed a bunch of beanbag chairs from the youth center and moved our staff meeting outside, changing the whole feel of the meeting.
- One week for our staff meeting, we decided to have lunch out of state. We headed for the Indiana border and let some dear Amish and Mennonite folks feed us. While we were out, we ran into a couple from the church. I told them we were working. And we were! We also had a lot of fun.
- Don Porter decided to turn one of our staff meetings into a malt shop. We brought in blenders and he made fruit smoothies. I was in charge of chocolate malts for the less health-conscious.
- We have taken staff retreats in the cottages of church members, started meetings with clips from *Everyone Loves Raymond* and *The King of Queens*, spent time singing together, and all sorts of other things.

The theme is always fun and creating space for life, joy, and laughter.

Over the years, we have tried to bring laughter into our worship experiences. You must understand that some people in the Midwest have strong feelings about how worship should look and sound. Their idea of reverence might not include belly laughs in the sanctuary. With this in mind, we have sensitively introduced humorous elements into our services.

One Sunday I was preaching a message on reaching out to our community with God's love. The passage for the message was, "'Come, follow me,' Jesus said, 'and I will make you fishers of men'" (Matt. 4:19). This is a serious topic. But we decided to try something creative. I asked Jim Bareman to give a fishing lesson. What you need to know about Jim is that he's an ordained elder in our church, a leader in our outreach ministry, a Sunday school teacher, and incredibly funny.

Jim walked up to the front of the church with credibility, respect, and his full fly-fishing outfit. He was wearing a huge hat covered with flies, and waders that came all the way up to his chest. He had a large flotation ring around his midsection and a rod that he swung just over the heads of the people who had gathered for worship. As he clomped his way up to the platform, he began to talk about fly fishing. He could barely be heard over the laughter, so he played it up.

But by the time he was done, the laughter had subsided and people were listening intently. He looked ridiculous, but his message about having the right equipment, fishing in the right place, and the importance of patience touched every heart in the room. In a sense, laughter opened people up so the message could go deep.

As the years have passed, people in our church have come to expect surprises in the worship services. I have often used movie clips that make a point and prompt laughter. One Sunday, while preaching on worship, I used a clip from one of my all-time-favorite comedies, *What about Bob?* In this scene, Bob is having dinner with the Marvin family. Bob has intruded on the family vacation of his therapist, and Dr. Marvin is not happy. While eating, Bob moans and groans with every bite. He enjoys his food with a level of sensual delight that Dr. Marvin's children and wife appreciate, but Leo Marvin does not. By the end of the clip, most of the people gathered for worship were cracking up. When I stood back up, I said, "That is how we should worship. No more halfhearted, phone-it-in, going-through-the-motions pseudoworship. We need to dig our teeth in, pour our hearts out, and not worry what the person sitting next to us is thinking about us."

Another Sunday I preached a whole message about laughter. We looked at the importance of humor and lightness of spirit and the need for Jesus' followers to let joy overflow. I used a short DVD piece developed by a creative Wesleyan Church in the Grand Rapids area. Daybreak Church had compiled a collection of clips of people laughing. It was beautiful—children and adults, men and women, eyes bright with joy, and laughter pouring out of their mouths and hearts. At one point, a woman in the DVD shifted from laughing to snorting; it was glorious. When the short piece was over, many in our worship center were laughing along.

One Sunday I got a little risky and illustrated a point with some visuals developed by the people at Despair, Inc. They call their line of pictures and posters "Demotivators." If you have ever seen the posters made by the Successories Company, you get the idea … sort of. Successories pairs beautiful pictures with positive sayings meant to lift people up. You have probably seen them displayed on office walls. The materials developed by the people at Despair, Inc., are the same, but different. The company markets itself (very tongue-in-cheek) as "makers of Demotivators, revolutionary tools for pessimists, underachievers, and the chronically unsuccessful." Their posters crack me up. Here are a few examples:

- The caption for a picture of a little penguin reads, "LIMITATIONS: Until you spread your wings, you'll have no idea how far you can walk."
- One poster features a piece of wood with lots of nails driven halfway in and bent badly in every direction. The caption reads, "INCOMPETENCE: When you earnestly believe you can compensate for a lack of skill by doubling your efforts, there's no end to what you can't do."
- On a poster with a stunning shoreline at sunset, we read, "MOTIVATION: If a pretty poster and a cute saying are all it takes to motivate you, you probably have a very easy job. The kind robots will be doing soon."

As I showed these posters to the congregation, I was reminded that humor is subjective. If you rush right to despair.com to look at the dozens of other posters, you probably have a sense of humor like mine. If you say, "Those posters don't seem very nice; I don't think they're very funny," you have some other kind of sense of humor. But as I said to the congregation that Sunday morning, find what makes you laugh and let it flow.

Over the years, I have tried to be a laughter-mentor to the staff I lead, the congregation, and even to my sons. I was proud beyond words when my youngest son, Nate, who has a sharp wit, gave me a framed print for Christmas. It's a picture of a gorgeous night sky with a shooting star blazing through the darkness. The text below the picture reads, "WISHES: When you wish upon a falling star, your dreams can come true. Unless it's really a meteorite hurtling to the Earth which will destroy all life. Then you're pretty much hosed no matter what you wish for. Unless it's death by meteor." What more can a father hope for?

Spend Time with Funny People

We can grow our souls and strengthen our ministries by spending time with people who make us laugh. We are wise to nurture relationships with people who have positive dispositions, overflow with the joy of Jesus, and know how to have fun.

Some years ago at a pastors conference, my wife, Sherry, and I were seated next to Wes and Claudia Dupin for a formal dinner. By the time the dinner was over, we had switched seats so that Sherry could talk with Claudia and I could converse with Wes. God quickly knit our hearts together and we have become great friends. When we are with the Dupins, and we get with them as often as possible, we pray together, speak of ministry plans and strategies, and always converse about ways to reach our community with the gospel. This is definitely an "iron sharpens iron" relationship. Yet somehow, in the middle of all the serious ministry conversation, we laugh. There have been times Sherry and I have driven away from a dinner with the Dupins and my stomach hurt from laughing. And I liked it.

One day Wes called and asked if the senior leadership team of Daybreak Church could come and spend an afternoon with Sherry and me. He wanted us to talk to them about helping the church build transition points for new believers to grow in their faith and connect in the life of the church. When we finished sharing our thoughts, Wes asked if the team could use my office for an hour to keep processing what they had learned. I said that would be fine and explained to Wes that before they left my office, they were each welcome to take one book from the "giveaway" section of my library. I showed them the four shelves filled with books I love to share with people.

I told them that when I was growing up, my doctor always had a box filled with colorful bracelets, spider rings, sugar-free gum, and other trinkets I could choose from before I left. I explained that I had the same program, only I give away books—one book for each person.

When I came into my office the next morning, all four shelves were empty. They had taken all of my books! Some time later, I found where Wes had hidden the books just to mess with my head. The next time we talked, Wes asked if anything was missing from my office when I came in the next day. I insisted, with a straight face, that everything was in order. When he told me about hiding my books, I let him think that the custodian must have found them and put them back before I came in. I didn't want him to know he got me, and he won't know, until he reads this chapter.

I've Got Your Back

Finding a Joy Mentor

I have a handful of people in my life who always bring me to a place of joy and laughter. I make it a point to regularly spend time with these people. There are moments when my soul feels depleted and I think I just might lose it. These people minister deeply to me. Such "joy mentors" play a unique role in a leader's life.

Identify the people God has placed in your life who bring you joy, lightness of spirit, and laughter. Make it a point to connect with these people frequently. And give them permission to tell you when you are taking yourself too seriously. Invite these people to play the God-given role of helping you lighten up when your sphincter gets too tight or you think the future of the church rests on your shoulders alone.

Laugh or Die

Grace leads to laughter, and laughter leads to grace. When we walk strongly in the grace of Jesus, we see ourselves clearly. We can admit our frailties, weaknesses, and points of need. We don't have to pretend we are perfect or have it all together. When we walk in the grace of Jesus, we can laugh with others and even at ourselves, because we know we are loved and are precious in God's sight, even with our weaknesses. In a similar way, laughter leads to grace. When we learn to laugh, when joy overflows our souls, Jesus is near.

Leaders must learn to laugh. We must laugh at ourselves, laugh with each other, and also laugh at some of the silliness we face in the work of the church. If we take everything we do seriously, we will wither up and die on the inside. If we can't open the pressure valve with laughter, we just might explode. So laugh or die. It's up to you.

The Revenge of Gus the Grunting Camel

The first snow of the season fell gently over western Michigan, covering the church parking lot with an inch of the fresh white stuff. When I walked outside, the air was crisp, fresh, and you could smell it — revenge was in the air. Josh Blunt, the instigator of the Gus the Grunting Camel episode, was about to experience the full fury of retaliation.

We had been in a church board meeting for most of the evening, and as I drove out the back parking lot, I noticed that someone had done a series of doughnuts all over the lot. I followed the tracks to the spot where Josh always parked. His office was near the children's department, so he was the only one who parked around the back. He had been at the late-night meeting, so the logical conclusion was that he had been racing and spinning around the parking lot before heading home.

Early the next morning, I called the office. It was Tuesday, normally my Sabbath day. So I asked Barb to email the staff, informing them that the police had been called late Monday night by an off-duty officer who had seen suspicious activity at the church — a dark SUV racing around the church, tearing things up. I had Barb inform the staff that one of our elders, who is also a sheriff, had driven to the church after midnight to investigate, and he affirmed that someone had been racing around the back parking lot doing doughnuts. There was no sign of a break-in.

Barb sent out a group email but verbally told everyone except Josh that it was just a prank. The first step was to see if Josh would confess.

Later that morning, Josh responded with his own email. He admitted to having done a few "controlled maneuvers, in a safe environment, away from the eyes of children" after the board meeting. He seemed to take the whole thing lightly and assured Barb that he was just testing his driving skills for the winter. His note was tongue-in-cheek, and he clearly did not see the gravity of the situation.

So we helped him get a fuller picture.

I wrote an email pretending to be Officer Huizenga (one of our elders), expressing great concern that a minister would take this kind of behavior so lightly. In the note, he expressed frustration that he got a call and had to come back to the church after midnight. Quite honestly, I laid it on pretty thick, but Officer Huizenga gave me permission. He was ready to play along.

Now Josh was feeling bad. He came to the office to talk with Barb and find out what the big deal was. She assured him that racing around the church parking lot, at any time, was no laughing matter. She even told him about how one of her boys had lost the privilege of using the school parking lot for a week after doing doughnuts at the high school. She let Josh know that she was pretty sure he would not lose his parking privileges at church, but you never know; this is serious stuff.

At this point, I started getting calls from some of the staff members who felt we ought to let Josh off the hook. I took charge and let everyone know that it would be good for Josh to sleep on this one.

The next morning, I got into the office and printed out the memo from Barb to the whole staff inquiring about the late-night activity in the parking lot, a copy of Josh's response, and a copy of Officer Huizenga's concerns. Then I hit my intercom button and, in as stern a voice as I could muster, asked Josh to come to my office. Josh entered sheepishly and sat down. I did not make eye contact with him but hit my intercom button and asked Don Porter to join us. He sat down and the fun really began.

I said, "Josh, I'm out for one day and when I get back I have this flurry of emails about how you were racing around the church property at all hours of the night doing dangerous maneuvers. Elders are called to the church after midnight to inspect the grounds. The police are calling. What in the world is going on?"

By this time, most of the staff had gathered just outside my door, which was slightly ajar. Josh went on to tell me the whole story, and he was apologetic. But he was confused over why this had become such a big deal. All he did was a few doughnuts. He was just having a little fun.

I assured him that little things can become a big deal in the life of the church. As he grew up as a leader, he would understand this. But for now, he was going to have to take my word for it. Then I reached over and hit my intercom button and asked Barb to bring in the new email that Officer Huizenga had sent.

I read the letter to Josh. It reinforced all I had been saying. It was signed, "Sincerely, Officer Larry Huizenga (GTGC)."

Then I asked Barb, "What does 'GTGC' mean?"

She said, "Oh, that's Gus the Grunting Camel."

I said, "Do you mean that letter was actually written by Gus?"

She assured me it was.

Josh began putting the pieces together. "You mean that letter was not from the police?"

I told him it was not.

"Then what about the other letter?"

We let him off the hook. It took a few minutes to sink in. Finally, I said, "Josh, the only thing in all of this that actually happened was that you did doughnuts in the parking lot. The rest is all an illusion."

He immediately cracked up and began to bow and say, "I'm not worthy! I'm not worthy!"

There is more to the story, and even more chapters will be written in the years to come. As we serve the Lord together, we will play, laugh, and take delight in a God who laughs with us. I hope you can laugh along and bring this kind of joy to your ministry.

chapter 8

Understanding and Harnessing Our Sexual Desires

The Leader's Libido

I know self-control is a fruit of the Spirit. Discipline is expected of those who lead the church. Yet I am just a person, with the same frailties, desires, and passions everyone else faces. Sometimes my eyes feast on images on a computer screen or TV set that shock me, yet I find it hard to look away. There are moments my emotional needs cry out, and if I am not careful, I can let the wrong person meet them. I seek to live with clear and God-honoring boundaries in my relationships, but the lines can become blurry. I know my sexuality is a good gift from God. Yet there are days when my desires seem too powerful to control. God, help me honor you with all of my life, including my sexuality.

> Flee from sexual immorality. All other sins a man com-
> mits are outside his body, but he who sins sexually sins
> against his own body. Do you not know that your body
> is a temple of the Holy Spirit, who is in you, whom you
> have received from God? You are not your own; you were
> bought at a price. Therefore honor God with your body.
>
> —1 Corinthians 6:18–20

> May your fountain be blessed, and may you rejoice in
> the wife of your youth. A loving doe, a graceful deer—
> may her breasts satisfy you always, may you ever be cap-
> tivated by her love.
>
> —Proverbs 5:18–19

It was a hard year. I received a one-two-three punch that knocked the spiritual wind out of me.

Punch one came when a dear brother, who had been in a pastors accountability group with me for many years, left his wife, children, and ministry for a woman in his church. He shocked the members of our group with a whole series of choices that turned his life upside down. Sadly, he never came to us early in the process, when his heart was wandering toward another woman. He told us after the damage had been done, the sexual lines had been crossed, and his ministry had been compromised. My initial response was anger. Our pastors group prayed with him and challenged him to seek restoration with his wife. But he rejected our council. We continue to pray for him and seek to keep the door of our lives open to him.

A few months later, I was hit with the second blow. I received a call from another pastor friend. "Can I come by your office to talk? I need to come over right now." I cleared my calendar for the morning. He walked into my office, sat in a chair, made no eye contact, and pensively looked at the floor. Finally, he spoke. "I have sinned. It could cost me everything. I don't even know how it happened, but I have sinned." I prayed for him and then listened. He explained that he had become involved with a woman, entered an emotional affair, and finally had a sexual encounter. When the woman found out he was a pastor, she blew the whistle. Again, I went through a strong emotional response. But this time, I was not angry. I was numb, confused, and filled with despair. Sadness came over me. I trusted this leader like a brother. I did not see this coming. I was brokenhearted for his wife, children, church, and for him. I mourned the effect his decisions would have on so many people. One bright light in this situation was that he committed to a process of confession and reconciliation.

The knockout punch came when I heard the accusations about Ted Haggard, president of the National Association of Evangelicals. Reporters were talking about "accusations" of his involvement with a male prostitute and illegal drug use. It seemed far-fetched, almost too bizarre. But something inside me broke. I had never met this pastor, but my gut told me that when the smoke cleared, things would be even worse than initially reported. This wasn't some kind of prophetic insight but feelings based on what I had been experiencing with my two pastor friends. I was growing painfully aware of the sinister power of sexual temptation.

Once the confessions came and things were in the light, I entered unfamiliar emotional territory. I was not angry, and I was not sad. I was filled with fear and profoundly introspective. Leader after leader was shipwrecking their lives through sexual compromise, and I had a sober awareness that I was not beyond temptation. I found myself scrutinizing my own ability to self-deceive, my propensity toward sin, how I can rationalize poor choices, and how I can live a double life if I'm not very careful.

Anger came when I realized my first friend was leaving his family and ministry for another woman. Sadness engulfed me as I walked with my second friend through his time of struggle. Sobering fear gripped me when the news broke on Ted Haggard. The fear has not gone away. I hope it never does.

Symptoms Check
My Desires Need Harnessing

☐ I find myself letting people in my church meet emotional needs that should be met only by my spouse.

continued ⇨

☐ I view movies, TV shows, internet sites, magazines, or other sources of visual stimulation in an effort to "meet my sexual needs." If these secret behaviors were to become public, I would be embarrassed and ashamed, and it might even compromise my ministry.

☐ I have created a fantasy world in my mind where I engage in sexual sin. I would never do these things in the real world, but I find myself playing out mental scenarios I know are wrong.

☐ I am living a double life. On the one hand, I call people to moral purity and holiness. But in my personal life, I engage in the very behaviors I condemn publicly.

☐ When the topic of setting relational boundaries comes up, I get defensive because I don't want to face the fact that I have a habit of crossing boundaries.

The Power of the Mind

I can't believe that three decades have slipped by since I grew up on Santa Barbara Street in Fountain Valley, California. As I write these words, I sit two thousand miles and a lifetime away from my childhood home. Yet at the speed of thought, I can close my eyes and find myself standing in our front yard. I can see the juniper shrubs, my best friend's house across the street, and the decorative giant Zs (one frontward and one backward) on our garage door.

I can see the hallway of our home—the strip of carpet my dad and mom made us run back and forth on when one of our feet fell asleep during dinner. It was torturous running on a prickly foot, but three or four times up and down the hall always did the trick. I can even smell the homemade chocolate fudge my mom made when we had company over. The scent still lingers, wafting through the storehouse of my mind.

The mind's power is staggering. It can transport us virtually anywhere in a flash. What we do with our minds, where we go, what we focus on, is critical for leaders. The mind can be a glorious place of hope, dreams, joy, and vision. It can also be a prison of lust, anxiety, and fear.

It's up to us.

Each of us can choose to harness our thought life and use it for God-honoring activities, or we can let it run wild and suffer the consequences. Like a spoiled child in a chocolate shop, if we let our thought lives consume whatever they want, we will end up ill, sitting in a pile of candy wrappers, wondering why we feel so sick when everything tasted so good.

Leaders don't have the luxury of living this way. Though every leader has weaknesses and struggles with sin, we are called to offer the full force of our mental capabilities to God. As we nurture our thought lives, we discover what it means to "love the Lord your God with all your heart and with all your soul and with all your mind" (Matt. 22:37).

Both leaders who are married and those who are single face this challenge. In a sex-saturated culture, we must guard our minds. This is the first line of defense. A leader whose outer world is squeaky clean can still allow the world of the mind to be perverse. The same mind that can catapult us back to a childhood home can create vivid sexual scenarios that dishonor God. Healthy church leaders inspect their thought lives and make sure they are seeking to live in holiness even in the hidden compartments of their minds.

Doctor's Insight
You May Not See It, but It's There

With a knowing look in his eyes, Dr. Dekkinga asked, "When did you notice the first problem with your skin?" I thought about it and said, "When I was thirty-six years old." Jack just nodded his head to confirm what he suspected.

continued ⟳

He explained that the kind of skin problems I have, the ones due to overexposure to the sun, tend to pop up about twenty years after the damage is done. He was exactly right. I had spent long days in the sun all my summers up to my sophomore year of high school. But for two decades, there was no sign of trouble. My skin was fine. There were no dry spots, recurring sores, or any indication of the serious consequences of my marathon days at the beach. Jack told me this is common.

If you had asked me, "Did all the years you spent in the California sun damage your skin?" I would have told you that I had gotten away with it. But I would have been wrong. The damage was there, and I was going to have to pay the proverbial piper. It's just that I was on a deferred payment program.

Leaders who battle with hidden sexual sin face the same reality. They might feel they have it covered up and that no one will ever know. Their private thought lives or viewing habits are just that—private! But just like skin cancer, they always come to the surface. The longer we ignore them, the worse things become.

The mind is a battlefield. If the enemy can dominate here, he can infiltrate, poison, and destroy every area of our lives. I discovered this struggle early in my life as a follower of Jesus. I was a student seeking to live out my faith on the campus of Orange Coast College. Every day was a challenge. I found my mind wandering places it should not have gone. There were attractive women in all of my classes and everywhere on the campus. Since we had endless summer, many wore beach clothes, and this only compounded the problem.

Help from My Friends

What Helps You Keep Your Motives and Life Pure?

My model for morality and integrity is my dad. He is a man of deep convictions and personal character. I have had regular conversations with him concerning what it means to live a moral life over the years. He constantly challenges me and provides a model of impeccable character.

My wife, Claudia, and I are open books with each other. If there is ever a question concerning any value, decision, or conduct, we ask each other.

My personal motivation is my two sons, whom I deeply admire and adore. When I'm tempted to go down the wrong road morally, I often ask myself, "How will this decision impact the lives of my sons?" This is a huge motivation for purity!

My board of elders meets regularly with me to ask the tough questions. This is not always comfortable, but it's extremely valuable.

My congregation is fully aware of my life. I am open with them concerning my values and integrity issues. I have never pretended to be perfect and will readily share my failures, struggles, temptations, and weaknesses. I share with them my personal choices concerning values and ethics.

— Wes Dupin, Senior Pastor, Daybreak Community Church, Hudsonville, MI

I wanted to devote my mind to higher purposes. But I had difficulty thinking about anything except women. I had been reading the gospels and was struck by how Jesus had battled the temptations of Satan by quoting Scripture (Matt. 4:1 – 11; Luke 4:1 – 13). If my

Savior used the Bible as a weapon against the attacks of the enemy, I would give it a try.

I decided to memorize a few verses from the book of 1 Peter. Each time my mind wandered, I would meditate on these verses. The first week, I found myself walking around the campus constantly muttering, "Peter, an apostle of Jesus Christ, to God's elect, strangers in the world ..." Honestly, it didn't help much.

I stuck with my commitment. If I was going to be a leader in the church, if I was going to live for God, I wanted my mind to be under his control and not running wild. So each time I found myself fixating on the lovely ladies of OC, I went back to 1 Peter. As one verse became part of my thinking and was rooted in my heart, I would add another.

To give you a sense of how much the battle raged and my eyes and heart wandered, over that year of college I memorized all five chapters of 1 Peter and also the book of Haggai. I did this not because I was disciplined but because I was desperate. At first, when my mind wandered to the wrong places, my response was mechanical. I would begin at 1 Peter, chapter one, verse one. I would rattle off the words as fast as I could. Even this remedial approach was helpful. Some of my lust-filled moments subsided, and I thought more about God's Word. But with time, something more substantial happened. The truth and power of God's Word filled and dominated my thought life. I slowly stopped dwelling on thoughts that dishonored God and poisoned my view of women. I began to reflect on the goodness of God, the value of people, the truth I was learning. I began praying for people on campus. My mind was being shaped by God's values and not the values of the world.

Through the year, something amazing happened. The battle subsided. It did not go away, but the intensity lessened. My mind focused, more and more, on thoughts that honor God. Believe me, it was not a quick fix. But with time, something inside of me changed. Close to three decades later, I still turn to meditating on Scripture when my eyes and mind wander where they should not be. Every time I do, the truth of God's Word brings power in the spiritual battle.

Memorizing passages of the Bible and reciting them might seem old-fashioned. Some see this as a discipline for grade-school kids trying to get stars on a chart in their Sunday school classroom. I disagree.

Doctor's Insight
Preventive Care

As I spoke with Dr. John Albrecht, my dentist, he began talking about the importance of preventive care. John explained that in the 1960s, a team from the University of Michigan had done studies on periodontal disease (gum disease) and learned that the primary cause was bacterial infection. At the time, there were relatively few dental hygienists. Most dentists would do a quick ten- to fifteen-minute cleaning of the teeth but would not address tartar under the gums.

Once the cause of periodontal disease was identified, preventive measures could be taken. Most dental hygienists now extensively clean and scrape the teeth at each appointment. They get under the gums and remove tarter so bacteria can't cling to it and attack the gums. Dentists encourage thorough brushing, but they know this cleans only about 60 percent of the tooth surface. So they educate patients on how to floss and clean the other 40 percent. When patients enter the preventive-care process, dental health increases. When they refuse to do their part, problems grow.

I believe the best way to practice preventive care of our souls, when it comes to sexual temptation, is to saturate our minds with God's Word. Meditating on Scripture is a cleansing process, and at any time, we can draw on portions of the Bible we have memorized.

The Wisdom of Setting Boundaries

Another way to keep from falling into sexual sin is by setting clear and God-honoring boundaries. Wise leaders understand that the most benign of relationships can become a problem if you don't set clear physical, emotional, and relational boundaries. This is something I gave a lot of thought early on in my ministry training.

The assignment was simple. Write a case study on some aspect of relationships in ministry. Each of us would present our papers the next time our seminary colloquy group met. I decided to address the issue of boundaries in ministry. As a young man doing ministry with high school students, I had established some boundaries that I found helpful, and I decided to discuss them in my case study.

Two weeks later, we met to present our cases. I had worked hard to list my boundaries and reasons for establishing them. I felt good about my paper. I really believed my presentation would be helpful and well received by the members of my colloquy group.

I was wrong.

I began by addressing the reality that all who serve in the church or in any Christian ministry face temptation. I made it clear that people in leadership roles have the responsibility to take great care not to fall to sexual temptation, and that we are also called to "avoid even the appearance of evil." The group members seemed resistant to these concepts, and their eyes let me know that they were not with me.

Then I presented the boundaries I had established in my youth ministry. First, I would never meet one-on-one with any of the young women in the youth group unless my wife or a church secretary was within earshot. The group members looked at me with skepticism. Next, I explained that I was careful not to be overly physical with the young women in the youth group. In particular, I told them that when I hugged the girls, I would do so with one arm, from the side, with what I had come to call a "buddy hug." I avoided the frontal hug. At this point, the group was glaring at me, but I pressed on. Apparently, my final boundary was the straw that broke the camel's back. I told them that I would never drop off a girl from youth group last, but I would go out of the way to drop a girl off first so that I was never in the car alone with any of the girls in the youth group.

At this point, one of the members of my colloquy group launched into me. "That is just ridiculous! You have got to be kidding!"

I didn't get the reasoned and thoughtful group discussion I had hoped for. Instead, the group members castigated me for being so rigid. They explained that I was entirely out of line and that my boundaries would actually get in the way of my ministry.

I looked to the professor, hoping for support. He focused on me with great concern in his eyes, chose his words carefully, and said, "I think you are afraid of your own sexuality."

I paused, thought long and hard, and said, "You better believe I am! I'm terrified of it!"

The silence was palpable.

Finally, one of the guys in the group spoke in a scolding way. "I am married, but my best friend happens to be a woman other than my wife. She is a fellow student here at the seminary. We spend time together one-on-one. I feel comfortable hugging her, and I don't see any problem with this." As I listened to him, I had a flashback to the first time I'd seen him on campus with his "best friend." I'd actually thought she was his wife and was shocked when I discovered she was not. It was clear to me that he was deeply infatuated with this woman and was drawing unhealthy attention from her.

Now I was ticked off.

I said, "Let me tell all of you something. In twenty years, I will still be in ministry. My boundaries might get in the way of some things, but they will also protect me from all kinds of pitfalls."

Two decades later, I am still in ministry. I also have a set of boundaries for my relationships with women, and they are even more rigid. If you were to ask me if I am still afraid of my sexuality, I would put it a little more gently than I did twenty years ago, but I would still say, "Yes, I am."

Help from My Friends
How Do You Establish Boundaries?

As a woman, my guideline is not to be alone with a man — especially a married man. I also keep appropriate boundaries — spiritually, emotionally, and physically. Even if I think it is not a problem, I try to avoid the potential for a problem.

continued ⟳

When I go to a good movie, but there is a scene that I sense I do not need to be seeing, I close my eyes (and sometimes my ears!) as the scene approaches. Occasionally, I just have to leave what I thought would be a good movie. Wrong images and words stick like barbs in my mind. I try to avoid the first contact. This goes for every form of media.

— Nancy Grisham, PhD, Evangelism Leader, Livin' Ignited

At Corinth Church, we address boundaries with our staff members. We have guidelines for how we relate to other staff members and people in the congregation. Here are some of the boundaries that are part of the staff culture:

- When a staff member meets with a person of the opposite sex, it needs to be in a room with a window or the door must remain open.
- Staff members can't meet after hours with a person of the opposite sex unless there are others in the building.
- Staff members may not meet one-on-one with a person of the opposite sex off church grounds.
- Generally, staff members do not drive in a car alone with a person of the opposite sex. (Obviously they can drive in groups or help someone in an emergency.)

No pastor or leader at Corinth would go out to lunch with a person of the opposite sex, either from the staff or the congregation. We feel this looks and feels too much like a date. Our staff and church board know that these boundaries are strict and that they can occasionally lead to complexities for travel and scheduling meetings. We also know these boundaries can't be absolutely rigid, that they are general guidelines. But we believe the benefits of clear boundaries far outweigh the drawbacks. And by God's grace, we have never faced a situation in which a staff member has ended up in a compromising relationship with someone on staff or with a church member.

I have friends in ministry whom I respect who feel the boundaries our church has set are too strict and would not work in their church cultures. My counsel is that they think through what is appropriate for their contexts, but that they set clear boundaries that protect their leaders, congregational members, and the name of Jesus.

The Power of Accountability

Along with meditating on Scripture and setting clear boundaries, wise leaders embrace accountability. This involves courage. It demands vulnerability. And it can save our lives.

A church leader asked if I could do him a favor. He said, "When I travel, I stay in hotels ... alone." He was having a hard time making eye contact but pressed on. "I ... well ... I have been watching movies that a Christian leader should not watch. I don't want to. I know it's wrong. But I am having a hard time stopping."

I asked him, "How can I help you?"

"Maybe, before I travel, I could tell you, and you could pray for me. Then when I get home, I could give you a report."

I told him I though he was very wise, and I committed to hold him accountable for two months. The next couple of trips, he resisted the temptation to watch inappropriate movies. When we hit the two-month mark, I asked if he felt he needed me to be the one to keep him accountable over the long haul. "No, I have a couple of close guy friends who would be great at this. I just came to you first because I knew you would not look down on me."

Help from My Friends
How Do You Seek Purity While Traveling?

When I travel in the West, I usually request that my hosts not put me in a hotel, unless I am traveling with my wife. This is because I find that in the West, even normal TV is often unedifying. Because I

continued ⇨

am very tired when I finish a day of ministry, I tend to put on the TV and watch for too long. If I must stay in a hotel, I usually ask for a roommate so that I will not be alone when I am tired after the battles of ministry. Generally, I prefer to stay in homes. The added advantage of staying in homes is that when I am in a foreign culture, I like as many opportunities as possible to identify with the people and get to know them. I know many preachers do not like the time spent talking. But I think it helps me get closer to people, and this helps me minister more effectively among them.

— Ajith Fernando, Director, Youth for Christ, Sri Lanka

The beauty of accountability is that we can tailor it to our needs. When we find a brother or sister we trust, we can ask them to keep us accountable in a very specific way. If our struggle is emotional attachment to someone in our ministry, we can have them pray for us and ask us if we are being careful to keep clear boundaries with this person. If our struggle is the hidden world of lust, we can invite an accountability partner to support us in prayer as well as ask us if we are keeping our thoughts heading in the right direction. If we are tempted with internet pornography, we can have a monthly report of all our internet activity sent to an accountability partner. Whatever

I've Got Your Back

Serious Accountability

I am part of two pastors support groups. These are not groups that meet to complain and gossip. They are groups where we get in each other's faces, share our lives deeply, pray passionately, and extend honest accountability. In one of the groups, we discussed internet pornography. As we expressed the challenges of staying pure in the world of our minds and avoiding this visual cesspool, we decided that each of us would subscribe to an internet reporting program that keeps a list of every site we access and then sends a monthly report to someone else in the group.

our need, a trusted friend who asks us the hard questions as well as encourages and prays for us is an amazing gift.

The Goodness of Sexuality

Christians should have great sex lives. In the context of marriage, of course. God created male and female and declared them "very good." The picture is compelling. A man and a woman in a beautiful garden—paradise! They were naked. They were not ashamed. God invited them to "be fruitful and multiply." When God created men and women, he intended for them to experience sexual intimacy. It is a good gift.

Christian leaders who want to honor Jesus need to embrace the goodness of God's creative plan. We need to celebrate the wonder, mystery, and passion of godly sex. For too long we have abdicated the realm of sexuality to the world. No more! It is time for God's people to recapture the world of sexuality.

Married leaders should make their sexual lives a high priority. Single leaders should live in sexual purity but still bless and celebrate the goodness of sex when it is expressed in the covenant relationship of a married man and woman. There are far too many church leaders who have decided that their sex lives will never be life-giving, joyful parts of their marriages, and they have become places of hidden pain and silent anger. When a ministry couple fails to embrace the goodness of their sexual relationship, it creates a rift between the husband and wife where the enemy of our souls can drive a wedge, creating a breeding ground for sexual temptation and indiscretion.

Most of the time, when a godly Christian man or woman begins crossing lines in the area of sexuality, it has to do with an emotional need. They feel far from their spouse. The rigors of ministry are taking a toll. The physical and emotional needs they carry deep inside begin to surface. Then someone comes along who will meet their emotional need. They are drawn to this person, first, because they "care about me." Once the emotional link has been established, sexual temptation begins to grow.

There is an amazing passage in Proverbs that addresses the goodness of sexuality, the call to fidelity, and the danger of sexual temptation. Read this passage closely. Catch the imagery of water as a picture of sexual intimacy:

> Drink water from your own cistern,
>   running water from your own well.
> Should your springs overflow in the streets,
>   your streams of water in the public squares?
> Let them be yours alone,
>   never to be shared with strangers.
> May your fountain be blessed,
>   and may you rejoice in the wife of your youth.
> A loving doe, a graceful deer —
>   may her breasts satisfy you always,
>   may you ever be captivated by her love.
> Why be captivated, my son, by an adulteress?
>   Why embrace the bosom of another man's wife?
> For a man's ways are in full view of the LORD,
>   and he examines all his paths.
>
> —Proverbs 5:15–21

The writer of Proverbs gives a series of warnings in the early section of chapter five. He calls us to avoid sexual temptation, to stay far away from those who seek to draw us in. He goes on to talk about the wisdom of receiving discipline and listening to the wisdom of others. We are called to ferocious fidelity and warned of the dangers of adultery. Yet in the middle of this serious caution comes a celebration of intimacy and sexual fulfillment.

All through the Bible there is a call for sexual celebration. Within the marriage covenant, there should be sexual blessing. Just as we are called to bless with our words, we are also called to bless with our bodies. Our genitalia, specifically, are to be fountains of overflowing blessing. The breasts, vagina, and penis are all part of the celebration of one-flesh intimacy. Romance and sexual intercourse are gifts from God to his people.

There is a clear sense in Scripture that we are to satisfy our spouses with our bodies. Read the words closely, and for heaven's sake, don't be embarrassed! "May her breasts satisfy you always." The passage could just as unashamedly say, "Let his penis satisfy you always." I know some will blush when they read these words. Some in God's family have relegated the realm of sexuality to a low place in life. They have missed the biblical reality that one-flesh sexual intimacy is a gift from their Creator.

When our sexual relationship is one that satisfies and our "fountain" is blessed, it leads to captivating love. Christian couples who make their sexual lives a priority discover that the emotional and physical desires that God has placed deep in their souls are satisfied. When we drink deeply from the fountain of marital intimacy, we no longer need our waters to be scattered in the streets. When our sex lives are healthy, growing, passionate, fulfilling, the need to look elsewhere drops significantly.

This is not to say that Christian leaders who have rich and fulfilling sexual relationships with their spouses won't face temptation. This is also not to say that those who enter into an inappropriate sexual relationship can somehow blame their spouse for not meeting their needs. But nurturing healthy sexual, romantic, and intimate relationships with our spouses will meet many of the needs God has placed inside of us. When we sense deep satisfaction and fulfillment in our sexual lives, we are quicker to recognize the counterfeit offers of the enemy and turn them down.

Network Building

Talk about It

If you are married, talk with your spouse about your romantic and sexual relationship. Use some of these questions to get the conversation started:

1. What are the things I do that make you feel close to me? What are things I do that make you feel distant from me?

2. How are we doing in nurturing a healthy romantic and sexual relationship?

3. How do you feel about the frequency of our sexual intimacy?

4. What do I do that brings you pleasure when we are sexually intimate and during intercourse?

5. What do I do that is not pleasing or makes you feel uncomfortable when we are sexually intimate and during intercourse?

If your sexual relationship with your spouse is broken or nonexistent, get help. Talk with a professional who can offer wisdom and help. When a car breaks down, we see a mechanic. When our computer crashes, we find someone who can recover the data. If your sexual relationship has hit a roadblock, don't accept where you are. Read a book, talk with a godly leader you trust, find a couple you respect and ask them to mentor you, see a counselor. Whatever you do, make sure this part of your life is healthy and strong.

Chapter 9

Bearing the Yoke of Jesus

The Leader's Back

People need me. How do I know? They tell me. I am called by God to be a leader in his church, but there are times, lots of times, I feel the job is too big for me. The needs are too deep. The responsibilities are too many. I try to bear the weight of the ministry, but there are moments the load seems too heavy. I bow down in prayer and under the sheer mass of what I have to do each day. Some days I feel the filling of the Holy Spirit making me strong in my weakness and I press on. Some days what I would really like to do is crawl into my bed and take a long nap — but that's not in my job description.

"Come to me, all you who are weary and burdened, and I will give you rest. Take my yoke upon you and learn from me, for I am gentle and humble in heart, and you will find rest for your souls. For my yoke is easy and my burden is light."

—Matthew 11:28–30

Then he said to them all: "If anyone would come after me, he must deny himself and take up his cross daily and follow me. For whoever wants to save his life will lose it, but whoever loses his life for me will save it."

—Luke 9:23–24

When I started in ministry, I swore it would not happen to me. I vowed to the God I serve that I would not let my life get out of balance. I had met too many bitter pastors' kids with stories about how they grew to hate the church because their pastor-parent lived with imbalance and let the church consume their family.

When I began in the ministry, I was determined not to let my family become another casualty washed up on the shores of ministry. When I got married, I established work habits that would allow me to give myself sacrificially to the church, which I believe is part of the Christian leader's calling, but I also made time for my wife. When we began having children, I again made sure there was margin for this new area of joyful responsibility. I was doing it right! I was making time for family, while still giving myself fully to the work of Jesus Christ.

While our family was away on vacation in Colorado one year, I experienced a wake-up call. Even though we were on vacation, I took work along with me. I was writing a small group Bible study on setting boundaries. I felt good about myself as I wrote and developed the discussion questions. The source material I was using was a sermon by Bill Hybels. In his message, he emphasized that he would serve at church only three to four nights a week.

I felt a little twinge of conviction because I had lots of nights filled with church work. I resolved that I would limit myself to four nights a week. I felt quite proud of this decision and mentioned it to Sherry. I said, "As I thought through my normal week, I realized that if I am not careful, I could end up back at the church every night of the week." My wife looked at me and said kindly but matter-of-factly, "You *are* back at the church every night of the week." I absorbed her words and then told her she was mistaken. She let me know that she was fairly sure she was right and that she and the boys really never expected me home in the evenings.

I was irritated by what felt like an insensitive accusation and scurried into the other room to get my Day-Timer to prove that she was wrong. I stood in the other room, Day-Timer in hand, and surveyed the previous month. I felt like I had been punched in the stomach. I had gone back to the office to work, every single night, for almost a month. Even on my day off, my Sabbath time of rest, I had scheduled meetings, counseling times, and other events that were "urgent" or "very important."

I wept. I was broken. I walked slowly back to the room where Sherry was reading. When she saw me, she knew something was wrong. It seems I was the only member of our family who was not aware my life had spun out of control. Sherry was gracious and forgiving. We talked, prayed, and planned together. I took my calendar and went through the coming month. I already had at least five or six nights of work scheduled every week for the coming month. But I promised Sherry, my boys, myself, and God that I would cut back to four nights a week.

I had to make phone calls when I got home and move some meetings and appointments. I learned to say no a little more often. I began a new way of living that would not break my back or destroy my family. I wrote the words "family night" three times each week to block off nights I would come home and stay home.

I knew I had to get serious about this commitment, so the next Sunday, in the pulpit, I told the whole story to the congregation. I asked them to forgive me for neglecting my wife and family. I invited them to pray for me and to keep me accountable to stay home at least three nights a week. Sherry wrote "family night" in big blue letters on the family calendar in the laundry room so the boys would know what nights I would be home.

The first official family night, I walked in the door from the garage and my youngest son jumped off the washing machine and onto my back. "Dad, you are staying home tonight, right?" I assured

I've Got Your Back

Go Home!

Set a goal for how much you feel it is responsible, in this season of your life, to work in your ministry. Specifically, set a cap on how many nights you will go back to church. Then invite your staff, board, and congregation to keep you accountable. Give them permission to send you home if you are overdoing it.

After I shared my story with the members of Corinth and told them of my commitment to be home three nights a week, people held me to it. Years later, people still remembered to ask me if I was honoring my family by being home enough.

him I was. He was overjoyed. Each family night, from that point on, Nate would be "hiding" on the washer and hurl himself onto me as I walked in. It became a highlight of my day. We all started looking forward to these nights together.

One evening, I walked in from the garage and braced myself for Nate to jump on my back. He wasn't there. I walked into the kitchen and called for the boys: "Zach, Josh, Nate ... family night!" Nothing.

Sherry called to me from another room. "The boys are all out doing things with friends."

I was shocked. "Didn't they know it's family night?"

"Yes, but they said you are always here!"

What a blessed and holy moment that was for me. I realized that my boys saw me as a dad who was home all the time. In grace, God

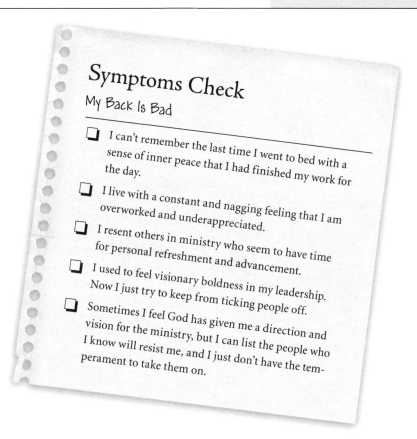

Symptoms Check
My Back Is Bad

☐ I can't remember the last time I went to bed with a sense of inner peace that I had finished my work for the day.

☐ I live with a constant and nagging feeling that I am overworked and underappreciated.

☐ I resent others in ministry who seem to have time for personal refreshment and advancement.

☐ I used to feel visionary boldness in my leadership. Now I just try to keep from ticking people off.

☐ Sometimes I feel God has given me a direction and vision for the ministry, but I can list the people who I know will resist me, and I just don't have the temperament to take them on.

had restored the damage I had done during the season my life was out of balance.

Bearing the Yoke of Jesus

To the overworked church leader, Jesus says, "Come to me, all you who are weary and burdened, and I will give you rest. Take my yoke upon you and learn from me, for I am gentle and humble in heart, and you will find rest for your souls. For my yoke is easy and my burden is light" (Matt. 11:28–30). We don't see yokes much these days. Jesus' metaphor in this passage is unfamiliar to us in our time and culture. But in the first century, everyone knew what a yoke was and the purpose it served. Yokes were custom-made by carpenters to fit on the back of an ox so the animal could be harnessed for work. The better the yoke fit, the more productive the ox would be.

William Barclay, a great Bible commentator, wrote that some carpenters in the first century may have hung signs outside their door that said, "My yokes fit well." Carpenters were highly skilled at making a yoke that would fit an ox just right. Barclay also notes that when Jesus said, "My yoke is easy," it could just as easily be translated, "My yoke fits well."

The concept is simple. Jesus knows exactly what burden you can bear. He is the master carpenter and has made a yoke that fits you perfectly. He knows what you should, and should not, carry. We get into trouble when we take up a yoke shaped by other people, or ourselves. Bearing Jesus' yoke requires sacrificial service, but as long as it is his yoke, it will fit right.

Jesus warns us to watch out for those who would load us up with heavy burdens. He talked about how the religious elite of his day were very comfortable with piling all kinds of loads on the people (Matt. 23:1–4). The same thing can happen today. If we aren't careful, we can end up crushed under the demands, expectations, and responsibilities people heap on us. We can even be guilty of overloading ourselves in an effort to please people or prove our own worth. No matter the source, being crushed under the weight of ministry is an indication that we are bearing the wrong yoke.

The call on every Christian leader is to receive, with humility, the yoke of Jesus. His yoke will always fit right. When we take the yoke of Jesus, we can carry the full burden that he has in mind for us, but it feels light. We will not be crushed under the weight because Jesus knows what we can handle.

Think about Jesus' description of how our lives will look when we follow him: "If anyone would come after me, he must deny himself and take up his cross and follow me. For whoever wants to save his life will lose it, but whoever loses his life for me will find it" (Matt. 16:24–25). Jesus' yoke looks a lot like a cross. The cross is heavy; it is an instrument of death; it is a place of reckoning. Yet it is the ultimate place of belonging and finding ourselves. When we take up the cross of Jesus, when we follow his way of life, when we embrace his teaching, the yoke is easy and the burden is light.

Healthy leaders don't carry the man-made burdens, yokes, and crosses imposed by those who believe they know God's plan for our lives. We come to Jesus and take his yoke. We discover that it always fits well. Our lives are full, ministry demands all the strength of the Spirit who dwells in us, we are driven to pray for the Father's help, but the burden seems light.

Self-Examination Suggestion
Whose Yoke Am I Carrying?

Reflect on your life and ministry. Are you bearing the yoke of Jesus? If you are, you will have a sense of peace and strength, even in the challenging times of ministry. Are you carrying a yoke fashioned for you by church members or your church board? If you are, you will feel overwhelmed, bitter, and resentful. Are you under a self-made yoke? If you are, the load might be too light and you could be coming short of God's vision for your life. Or the load could be enormous and crushing. If you sense that you are carrying any yoke other than the one Jesus has for you, it's time to make a change.

Reclaiming a Forgotten Gift of Grace

When God created the heavens and the earth, he gave us an example to follow. After six days of labor, God rested. God took a day off. He was not tired, but he was modeling a rhythm of life for us to follow. Later, God raised the value of taking a Sabbath when he gave the Ten Commandments. Healthy church leaders are secure enough to embrace Sabbath and walk away from their work for one day each week.

Each time we take a Sabbath, we make three declarations to heaven, earth, our church, and ourselves.

1. We trust that God is capable of running the universe and his church without us.
2. We are confident that God can provide all we need in six days of labor.
3. We understand that slowing down and meeting with God and his people is a priority in our lives.

As leaders, we can't call people to experience the joy and strength of rest if we aren't modeling this practice. Leaders who refuse to take a full day off each week make a profound theological statement: I am more powerful and important than God. Does that sound overstated? Think about it. God, who is omnipotent, took a Sabbath and called you to do the same. You, who are limited, refuse to take a Sabbath day. What message are you declaring by this behavior?

Network Building

Corinth Church has multiple staff. With this in mind, we coordinate to make sure everyone gets a Sabbath while still covering all the bases. We have been able to schedule people's days off so that the needs of the church are met and each leader can really enjoy the day without getting calls. Of course, if there is an emergency, people are ready to serve, but for the most part, the day is guarded. My Sabbath has been on Tuesday for almost all of my ministry, and I love this day.

Solo pastors may feel that they can't really experience a Sabbath. But if we understand that the church is a priesthood of all believers (1 Peter 2:5, 9), we know that others in the body can meet the needs of the congregation. If we follow the call to "prepare God's people for works of service" (Eph. 4:12), we will have a team of gifted church members ready to serve when we are not available.

My wife and I were teaching a seminar at the National Pastors Convention titled "Making Marriage and Ministry Complement and Not Compete." It was an eight-hour Critical Concerns Course held during a two-day period. One of the topics we addressed was the need to carry an appropriate burden in ministry. We called the leaders taking the course to live a balanced life that would lead to a healthy long-term ministry.

In particular, we addressed the importance of taking a Sabbath, not to heap one more layer of legalism on already burdened lives but to help them discover the freedom of rest. We emphasized that leaders must follow the rhythm of heaven and the heart of God by taking one day out of every seven to step back from their ministry labors. We both noticed a number of wives jabbing their husbands in the ribs as if to say, "Listen up!"

Help from My Friends

What Do You Do to Keep Your Soul Healthy and Fresh?

I practice a Sabbath every Friday. This is extremely important to my sanity.

Every summer, I take a four- to six-week study break far away from my church and the community I serve. Often during the third or fourth week, God begins to deal with hidden resentment, sin, and junk in my life that has accumulated during the previous year. This has been one of the most valuable gifts my church has given me over the past seventeen years.

Every summer, I go with a small group of guys to do some extreme hiking. The closeness to God's creation and spending great time with godly men has cleansed my soul in special ways.

— Wes Dupin, Senior Pastor,
Daybreak Community Church, Hudsonville, MI

One of the men in the group blurted, "What if my church won't let me take a Sabbath?" I asked him to explain. He said that his church members, and the board, expected him to work and be on call all the time. The idea of a day off, a Sabbath, was not in their understanding of a pastor's role.

My response surprised him and, quite frankly, surprised me. I asked, "What would you do if your church members and board told you that they expected you to commit adultery as part of your job description?"

He declared, "I would tell them no!"

I asked, "Why?"

As he answered, he got the point. The same God who commanded that we not commit adultery also ordained the Sabbath day. We had a rich conversation about whom we serve. We came back to the basics that we serve God first, not the whims of a church board or demanding people. Really, we were coming back to the issue of whose yoke we wear.

Leaders who want to stay healthy and serve God for a lifetime look into Jesus' face and discover that he is a Good Shepherd, not a harsh taskmaster. The God we love and serve calls us to bear his yoke, which will always fit right. Even in times that demand sacrifice and hard work, our Savior reminds us that he "makes me lie down in green pastures, he leads me beside quiet waters, he restores my soul" (Ps. 23:2–3).

Concluding Thoughts

Personal Journal, January 14

As I sit writing the final words of this book, I have fourteen stitches across my forehead.

About a month ago, during one of my weekly skin exams, I noticed a spot above my right eyebrow that seemed "suspicious," as the doctors say. It was pink, soft, and sore. I called my dermatologist's office and set up an appointment. A biopsy identified the spot as another basal cell carcinoma. This is fairly mild stuff, as long as you deal with it right away. So we set a date for another Mohs procedure.

Last week, right in the middle of my push to finish this book, I went to see Dr. Dekkinga. They numbed my forehead with about six or seven shots, and Jack carefully cut out a piece of my skin about the size of a dime. Then they carefully sewed me up and sent me home.

In a couple of days, I will go back to the doctor's office, and they will remove the stitches. I will thank them: the nurses, the ladies in the office, and most of all, Jack. It seems strange to thank someone for cutting out a piece of your forehead, but I am thankful. He has taught me how to practice self-exams each week so we can catch problems when they are small. He has instructed me to have Sherry examine my back because I can't see the problems that might be developing there. And when skin issues arise, he is ready to help me with the best solution. All of these lessons about my skin have taught me profound spiritual truths.

I am thankful for what God is teaching me along the way. I am convinced that I must lead from the inside out. I need to be tenaciously committed to regular and thorough self-exams of my soul and every aspect of my life. If I want to remain healthy as a leader, I need to invite people I trust to watch my back and let me know when they see problems developing.

The process will be hard at times.

It will leave scars.

I will need humility and courage.

But it will all be worth it when I hear, "Well done, good and faithful servant."

Discussion Questions and Prayer Prompters

Introduction

The Life-Giving Power of Self-Examination

1. Read Psalm 26:2–3; Lamentations 3:40; and 2 Corinthians 13:5–6. The Bible makes it clear that self-examination is important for every follower of Christ. Why do you think so many leaders don't practice self-examination?

2. What are some of the consequences of leaders' failing to live examined lives?

3. Describe a time when one of your choices or actions had harmful repercussions. If you had known the full impact of your actions, what would you have done differently?

4. Read the section "Turning Patients into Dermatologists" on page 15. How can this lesson be applied to our spiritual lives and ministries?

5. On page 16, we read, "Your personal choices are never just personal; your choices and the condition of your inner life impact others." If you make a poor choice, who are some of the people your decision could affect?

6. Name a church leader who leads an examined and healthy inner life. How has the integrity of this person's inner life impacted his or her ministry, family life, and friendships?

7. Name one person who has permission to raise concerns or hard issues with you. How has this person made you a better leader?

8. If you have ever been part of an accountability group, how has this experience shaped your life and ministry?

Prayer Prompters

Use one or more of the following suggestions to pray as a group:

1. God, forgive me for the times I have neglected to practice self-examination and help me begin a new season of diligence in this area of my spiritual leadership life.
2. Give thanks for the healthy leaders who have influenced you.
3. Ask for the courage to let others come close enough to keep you accountable on a deeper level.

Chapter 1

The Leader's Heart

1. Read the journal entry on page 23 and the "Symptoms Check" on page 25. On a scale of 1 – 10 (1 being a faint heartbeat and 10 being strong and healthy), how would you rate your heart? What causes your heart to weaken? What causes it to grow strong?
2. Tell about one or two disciplines that have helped you keep your heart for God beating strong.
3. Read the "Self-Examination Suggestion" on page 33. There is a little of Wallace, the nobles, and Longshanks in each of us. How have each of these kinds of leadership surfaced in your heart and ministry?
4. On page 34, we read, "There is no better place to learn the art of forgiveness than in the life of the church. The church is filled with people. People are broken and sinful. Spend enough time in the church and you will be hurt." How have you experienced both personal hurt and the need to forgive through your years of ministry?
5. Name one person you care about who doesn't know the love of Jesus. How are you seeking to reach out

to this person with the gospel? How can your group members pray for you and support you as you invest in this relationship?

6. The demands and challenges of ministry can yank leaders out of the world and force them to spend their time almost exclusively with believers. What do you do to keep yourself connected with lost people? How do you resist the gravitational pull of the church so that you are able to connect meaningfully with people who are still far from God?

Prayer Prompters

Use one or more of the following suggestions to pray as a group:

1. God of compassion, soften my heart and fill it with love like yours. Help me take steps to strengthen my heart so that it overflows with love for ...
2. Confess anything that has become a first love, and ask for your heart to beat with a new devotion to God.
3. Lift up prayers of blessing and thanks for group members.
4. Think of a person you care about who doesn't know Jesus. Ask the Holy Spirit to open and soften this person's heart, and pray for direction as you seek to be a witness to God's love.

Chapter 2
The Leader's Mind

1. Read Philippians 4:8 and Psalm 119:97–98. What is the common message of these passages?
2. What are some of the things that can derail your thought life and keep you from focusing on things that honor God and strengthen your faith?
3. Read the "Symptoms Check" on page 42. What symptoms do you see in your life?

4. How well are you prioritizing personal study of God's Word (not sermon preparation or church work, but time for you to invite the Spirit to shape your mind)? What is one step you can take to deepen your commitment to growing your mind through studying God's Word?

5. Name someone who has inspired you to keep learning and growing your mind. How has this person influenced you?

6. Referring to the avenues listed on pages 53–54, describe how you are seeking to be a lifelong learner. Share with the group any creative or life-changing learning processes you have experienced.

7. Give a synopsis of a book that has challenged your thinking and strengthened your ministry. If you have a list of must-read books, share it with the group.

Prayer Prompters

Use one or more of the following suggestions to pray as a group:

1. Spirit of God, fill and expand my mind. Help me to do my part to sharpen it. Give me a love for your Word and a hunger to keep learning all the days of my life.

2. Thank God for the mind he has given you. Commit to use your mental faculties for his glory.

3. Thank God for the writers, teachers, leaders, artists, and others who have influenced your thinking and stretched your perspective on life and faith.

4. Pray for diligence as you seek to develop mind-growing habits.

Chapter 3

The Leader's Ears

1. Read the journal entry on page 59. How would one of your church members describe your ability to really hear them when they speak? How would God describe

your ability to hear and respond to his voice and his leading in your life?

2. Read John 10:1–4. What do you learn about shepherds and sheep in this passage? If Jesus is the shepherd and we are his sheep, what is Jesus teaching about our ability to recognize and follow his voice?

3. Tell about a time you followed God when you heard him speak, felt his prompting, or received direction for your life. What resulted from your obedience?

4. If you could meet with any church leader within driving distance and spend time picking his or her brain, whom would you meet with and what would you ask?

5. How do you discern the difference between a person who is attacking you with unhealthy criticism and someone who is bringing helpful critique?

6. Read the "Help from My Friends" on page 77. How might you use these principles for getting honest feedback in your ministry?

7. Identify one action you can take to improve your hearing.

Prayer Prompters

Take a ten-minute time of silence so each member of your group can ask God one or more of the questions listed in the "Self-Examination Suggestion" on page 63. After this time of listening, share with your group something God has placed on your heart.

Chapter 4

The Leader's Eyes

1. Tell about a time you had an experience like Elisha's servant and were allowed to see some aspect of the spiritual world. How did this transform your perspective?

2. What is one spiritual battle you are facing in your ministry? How can your group members pray as you seek to stand strong?

3. Tell about a person in your life who has the gift of spiritual discernment. How does God use his or her gift to support and strengthen your ministry?

4. What could you do to learn from your church's history? How can you bless what God has done in the past?

5. Where is God at work in your community or ministry? What might you do to help your church step into the flow of where the Spirit is working?

6. What short-term goal do you believe God wants your church to address? What needs to happen for this vision to become a reality?

7. What long-term vision has God given your church? What needs to happen for this to become a reality?

Prayer Prompters

Use one or more of the following suggestions to pray as a group:

1. Open my eyes to see you with growing clarity. Lift the veil so that I might see your power and presence.

2. Pray for the members of your group as they face spiritual battles.

3. Thank God for the history of your church. Whether it's two years or two hundred years old, God has been at work. Give him glory for what he has done.

4. Pray for the future of your church. Ask God to lead you with new clarity and passion.

Chapter 5

The Leader's Mouth

1. Read Proverbs 12:18–19, 25; 16:21; and 18:21. What do you learn about the power of your words?

2. Tell about a person who consistently encourages and blesses you with their words. How has God used this person in your life?

3. What are some indicators that a culture of blessing is growing in your church? What steps can you take to help your church develop a stronger culture of blessing?

4. What could you do to encourage and affirm other church leaders in your community?

5. How well does your church live out Jesus' teaching in Matthew 18:15–17? How can you help your church become a no-gossip zone?

6. Without using names, tell about a time you spoke the truth in love and the person received what you said and grew as a result.

7. What are some of the consequences a church will face if a leader refuses to speak the truth in order to avoid conflict or hurt feelings?

Prayer Prompters

Use one or more of the following suggestions to pray as a group:

1. God of creation, you made my mouth. You know the potential for my words to heal or destroy. Please help me control my words and use my mouth to ...

2. Thank God for the people he has placed in your life who have used their words to bring you encouragement and strength.

3. Pray against the enemy's efforts to plant the seeds of gossip and a complaining spirit in your church.

4. Lift up prayers of praise for other ministries and leaders in your community.

Chapter 6

The Leader's Hands

1. Think about how Jesus used his hands when he healed and served people. Picture the hands of Jesus when he was hanging on the cross. Now look at your hands.

How do you want your hands to be more like the hands of Jesus?

2. In Jesus' day, foot washing was a common and humble act of service. What are some contemporary ways church leaders adopt a posture of humble servitude?

3. How can you walk the fine line between delegating responsibilities yet continuing to grow as a humble servant?

4. Who in your church has an A-WICS attitude? How does God use this person to inspire deeper levels of service in the lives of others?

5. On pages 127–28 are examples of how a church can serve other congregations in its community. What are some of the ways your congregation is serving in your community? What is one way your church could offer resources, support, and service to another congregation?

6. Tell about a Christian who mentored you and invested time, wisdom, and love in your spiritual development. What does this person mean to you?

7. Identify one person God has called you to mentor. How is God using you to shape this person into an effective leader?

Prayer Prompters

Use one or more of the following suggestions to pray as a group:

1. Jesus, I thank you for touching people and healing them, for washing feet, and for allowing the nails to be driven into your hands. I give you my hands and ask you to make me a servant like you.

2. Thank God for people in your church who serve with passion and faithfulness.

3. Pray for your congregation to commit to serve the community where God has placed you.

4. Ask God to lead your church to a place of joyfully serving other congregations.

Chapter 7
The Leader's Funny Bone

1. Read Proverbs 15:13 – 15; Nehemiah 8:10; and Psalm 126:2. Why do you think God wants his people to experience joy, cheer, and laughter? What keeps leaders from experiencing the fullness of God's joy?
2. Tell about a time you saw the power of laughter break down walls and bring people together.
3. If you have a funny ministry story, share it with the group.
4. How does your staff create space for play, expressions of joy, and laughter? What is one way you can raise the laughter quotient in your staff or leadership gatherings?
5. Describe your church worship experiences and how joy-filled laughter might fit in. What are some of the ways you make space for humor and laughter in congregational worship?
6. If you have a joy mentor, tell the group about this person and how he or she brings joy to your life.
7. On page 147, we read, "Grace leads to laughter, and laughter leads to grace." How are grace and laughter connected?

Prayer Prompters

Use one or more of the following suggestions to pray as a group:

1. Thank God for the privilege of play, the gift of joy, and the release of laughter.
2. Pray for your church to be known for overflowing joy.
3. Thank God for the people he has placed in your life to teach you how to play and laugh.
4. Lift up those people in your church who believe God spends his time sucking on lemons. Ask for a spiritual breakthrough in their lives so that they can experience the joy of the Lord.

Chapter 8

The Leader's Libido

1. What emotions do you experience when a news reporter announces the fall of another prominent Christian leader?

2. Read Proverbs 5:15–21. What warnings does this passage give about sexuality? What affirmations do you find in this passage?

3. Read the "Doctor's Insight" on page 155. My dermatologist taught me that skin problems will often surface two decades after the damage has been done. How is this true when it comes to hidden sins like lust, viewing pornography, or illicit sexual relationships? What would you say to leaders who believe their "secret" sexual sins will not impact their ministries?

4. Much of the battle with sexual sin is fought in the mind. What practices and ideas have you learned for keeping your mind pure?

5. Tell about any boundaries you have set to help you avoid temptation and "the appearance of evil." Also, tell the group about any formal boundaries your church has set for staff members' conduct with people of the opposite sex.

6. How could your group members pray for you and keep you accountable in the area of sexual purity?

7. How has the church dropped the ball on embracing and celebrating the gift of sexuality? What steps can we take to reclaim this good gift?

Prayer Prompters

Use one or more of the following suggestions to pray as a group:

1. Pray for those who have fallen into sexual temptation and sin, including you. Ask God to help leaders stand strong and resist the many temptations they face.

2. Thank God for the good gift of human sexuality.

3. Pray for the church to have the courage to claim sexuality as God's wonderful gift and to call people to purity.
4. Pray for the members of your group to experience the full blessing of being male or female. At the same time, pray for them to set boundaries that protect them from sexual sin.

Chapter 9

The Leader's Back

1. Tell about a time you felt the weight of ministry was too much for you to carry. What got you to this point? How did you move beyond it?
2. Read Jesus' words in Matthew 11:28–30 and Luke 9:23–24. How do these texts seem to contradict each other? How do they complement each other?
3. If you have experienced a season in ministry when your schedule spun out of balance, describe how this happened. What did you do to get things back in balance? If your life is out of balance now, what will you do to correct this?
4. In what ways do you embrace and celebrate a weekly Sabbath? What day do you take off from your ministry responsibilities? What do you do on this day to refresh your soul?
5. If you don't observe a Sabbath, explain why it is hard for you to walk away for a day. If you take a day off but always feel compelled to drop by the office, check your email, or make a few church-related phone calls, why do you do this?
6. As you look at your life and ministry, which of the following would you say you are carrying?
    • A yoke you have placed on yourself.
    • A yoke church people have put on you.
    • The yoke of Jesus.
    • A combination of the options above.

What do you need to do to lay down every other yoke so you can carry the yoke of Jesus?

Prayer Prompters

Use one or more of the following suggestions to pray as a group:

1. Thank Jesus for bearing the cross for you.
2. Praise God for the privilege of serving his bride, the church.
3. Confess where your life has spun out of balance, and pray for the wisdom and strength to carry only the yoke of Jesus.
4. Ask for the humility and discipline to observe a weekly Sabbath.
5. Pray for the discipline to practice self-examination in every area of your life.

Notes

Introduction: The Life-Giving Power of Self-Examination

20 *This sketch of Corinth Church ...* For more information, check www.corinthreformed.org.

Chapter 1: Love Strengthens Every Relationship

26 *Sherry Harney, author and speaker.* Yes, this is my wife.

Chapter 2: Lifelong Learning Expands Our Horizons

47 *Nancy Grisham, PhD, Evangelism Leader, Livin' Ignited.* For more information on Nancy's ministry, see www.livinignited.org.

49 *Bob Bouwer, Senior Pastor, Faith Church, Dyer, IN.* For more information on Faith Church, go to www.faith-churchonline.org.

53 *... one of the influential forces in my writing the book* Seismic Shifts. For information on doing a Seismic Shifts Church Campaign, see www.seismicshifts.com. For additional resources, see the blog www.seismic-shifts.blogspot.com.

53 *We live in a day in which there are more conferences available ...* There are many wonderful conferences, but some of my favorites are the National Pastors Convention, the National Outreach Convention, and the Willow Creek Leadership Summit.

54 *Supplement your diet of books ...* I find the following magazines helpful: *Christianity Today, Leadership,* and *Rev.*

Chapter 3: Attentive Listening Informs Wise Decisions

64 *Kim Levings, Director, Outreach Ministries.* Kim has been a leader with the Outreach organization for

many years and helped pioneer the development of the National Outreach Convention. The Outreach Media Group website is www.outreachmediagroup.com.

Chapter 4: Clear Vision Sees What Lies Ahead

87 ... *a dynamic and community-transforming church in Paramount, California.* This church is now led by Harold's son Ken. It continues to be one of the best examples of a biblical church that I have ever seen. For information on this dynamic ministry, go to www. emmanuel-church.org.

87 *"Bless their past ..."* I checked with Harold to make sure I accurately remembered what he said. (I heard it more than two decades ago.) Harold confirmed I remembered it correctly and gave me permission to quote him.

Chapter 5: Affirming Words Bring Blessing and Energy

104 ... *from Pastor Sam, from Grand Rapids First Church.* For more information on Grand Rapids First Church, go to www.grandrapidsfirst.org.

111 *Ajith Fernando, Director, Youth for Christ, Sri Lanka.* I highly recommend Ajith's book, *Jesus Driven Ministry,* published by Crossway Books. Ajith has led the Bible study at the Urbana gathering three times and is one of the finest biblical expositors I have ever read or heard.

113 *When Adam Barr came to Corinth ...* Adam now leads Borderlands Ministries. For more information, go to www.borderlandsweb.com.

114 *As I sat with Dr. Baxter ...* This is the only pseudonym I've used for the doctors mentioned in this book. Because his report was somewhat negative, he didn't want his name used.

115 ... *people spoke of the "marks of the true church."* In the Reformed Church in America, the denomination I

serve, we have guidelines for church discipline laid out in our *Book of Church Order*. Although there are some challenges to being part of a denomination, one of the great gifts is the structure and direction offered in many areas of ministry, including church discipline.

Chapter 6: Humble Service Reveals Jesus' Presence

120 *It was Easter Sunday* ... This story was told by Robert H. Schuller to a group of leaders at the Crystal Cathedral more than twenty years ago. My account of the story is how I remember his telling it, not necessarily how it happened.

Chapter 7: Laughter Sustains Our Sanity

136 ... *the Leadership Network Young Leaders Gathering* ... Little did I know, way back then, that I would one day write a book in a series developed by Leadership Network. You are holding that book in your hands right now. Over the years, I have gained great insight from resources developed by this organization, and I encourage you to read the back of this book for more information.

139 ... *Emily from Bronner's Christmas Wonderland* ... Although Emily doesn't exist, there is actually a Bronner's. I am certain their sales staff is very polite and that they do not have camels that can grunt out "Silent Night." You can find them at www.bronners. com.

140 ... *punk'd, X'd*. These are terms used on two TV shows that play practical jokes on people.

143 ... *a short DVD piece developed by a creative Wesleyan Church* ... Daybreak Church creates all sorts of creative resources for worship and also holds a dynamic gathering called the Creative Infusion Conference. For more information, go to www.daybreak.tv for

the church and www.daybreak.tv/conference for the
Creative Infusion Conference.

144 *They call their line of pictures and posters "Demotivators."*
If you have a sense of humor like mine, call a few
friends and log on to www.despair.com.

Chapter 8: Understanding and Harnessing Our Sexual Desires

157 *Wes Dupin, Senior Pastor, Daybreak Community
Church, Hudsonville, MI.* For more information on
Daybreak Church, go to www.daybreak.tv.

Chapter 9: Bearing the Yoke of Jesus

170 *... a sermon by Bill Hybels.* These studies eventu-
ally became a guide in a small group series called
Interactions, published by Zondervan and Willow
Creek.

174 *William Barclay, a great Bible commentator ...* This is
found in Barclay's Daily Study Bible Series, published
by Westminster Press.

Suggested Reading

Many books and resources can help you dig deeper into the topics discussed in this book. Here are some suggestions:

Blackaby, Henry T., and Claude V. King. *Experiencing God.* Broadman and Holman, 1994.

Cloud, Henry, and John Townsend. *Boundaries Face to Face.* Zondervan, 2003.

Foster, Richard. *Celebration of Discipline.* Harper and Row, 1978.

Frazee, Randy. *Making Room for Life.* Zondervan, 2003.

Harney, Kevin. *Seismic Shifts: The Little Changes That Make a Big Difference in Your Life.* Zondervan, 2005.

Ingram, Chip. *Love, Sex, and Lasting Relationships.* Baker, 2003.

Ortberg, John. *The Life You've Always Wanted.* Zondervan, 1997.

Piper, John. *A Godward Life.* Multnomah, 1997.

Stanley, Charles. *How to Listen to God.* Thomas Nelson, 1985.

Thomas, Gary. *Sacred Pathways.* Zondervan, 2000.

See also the list of books in the table on page 56.

About the Leadership Network Innovation Series

Since 1984, Leadership Network has fostered church innovation and growth by diligently pursuing its far-reaching mission statement: *To identify high-capacity Christian leaders, to connect them with other leaders, and to help them multiply their impact.*

While specific techniques may vary as the church faces new opportunities and challenges, Leadership Network consistently focuses on bringing together entrepreneurial leaders who are pursuing similar ministry initiatives. The resulting peer-to-peer interaction, dialogue, and collaboration—often across denominational lines—helps these leaders better refine their individual strategies and accelerate their own innovations.

To further enhance this process, Leadership Network develops and distributes highly targeted ministry tools and resources, including books, DVDs and videotapes, special reports, e-publications, and free downloads.

Launched in 2006, the Leadership Network Innovation Series presents case studies and insights from leading practitioners and pioneering churches that are successfully navigating the ever-changing streams of spiritual renewal in modern society. Each book offers *real* stories, about *real* leaders, in *real* churches, doing *real* ministry. Readers gain honest and thorough analyses, transferable principles, and clear guidance on how to put proven ideas to work in their individual settings.

With the assistance of Leadership Network—and the Leadership Network Innovation Series—today's Christian leaders are energized, equipped, inspired, and enabled to multiply their own dynamic kingdom-building initiatives. And the pace of innovative ministry is growing as never before.

For additional information on the mission or activities of Leadership Network, please contact:

LEADERSHIP NETWORK®

800-765-5323 • www.leadnet.org • client.care@leadnet.org

The Leadership Network Innovation Series

Confessions of a Reformission Rev.

Hard Lessons from an Emerging Missional Church

Mark Driscoll

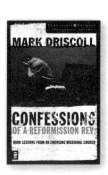

This is the story of the birth and growth of Seattle's innovative Mars Hill Church, one of America's fastest growing churches located in one of America's toughest mission fields. It's also the story of the growth of a pastor, the mistakes he's made along the way, and God's grace and work in spite of those mistakes.

Mark Driscoll's emerging, missional church took a rocky road from its start in a hot, upstairs youth room with gold shag carpet to its current weekly attendance of thousands. With engaging humor, humility, and candor, Driscoll shares the failures, frustrations, and just plain messiness of trying to build a church that is faithful to the gospel of Christ in a highly post-Christian culture. In the telling, he's not afraid to skewer some sacred cows of traditional, contemporary, and emerging churches.

Each chapter discusses not only the hard lessons learned but also the principles and practices that worked and that can inform your church's ministry, no matter its present size. The book includes discussion questions and appendix resources.

> "After reading a book like this, you can never go back to being an inwardly focused church without a mission. Even if you disagree with Mark about some of the things he says, you cannot help but be convicted to the inner core about what it means to have a heart for those who don't know Jesus."
>
> — Dan Kimball, author, *The Emerging Church*

> "… will make you laugh, cry, and get mad … school you, shape you, and mold you into the right kind of priorities to lead the church in today's messy world."
>
> — Robert Webber, Northern Seminary

Softcover: 0-310-27016-2

The Multi-Site Church Revolution

Being One Church in Many Locations

Geoff Surratt, Greg Ligon, and Warren Bird

Fueled by a desire to reach people for Christ, a revolution is underway. Churches are growing beyond the limitations of a single service in one building. Expanding the traditional model, they are embracing the concept of one church with more than one site: multiple congregations sharing a common vision, budget, leadership, and board. Drawing from the examples of churches nationwide, *The Multi-Site Church Revolution* shows what healthy multi-site churches look like and what motivates congregations to make the change. Discover how your church can:

- cast a vision for change
- ensure a successful DNA transfer (vision and core values) to its new site
- develop new leaders
- fund new sites
- adapt to structure and staffing change
- use technology to support its worship services

You'll identify the reasons churches succeed and how they overcome common snags. *The Multi-Site Church Revolution* offers guidance, insights, and specific action steps as well as appendixes with practical leadership resources and self-diagnostic tools.

> "I wholeheartedly recommend this book for any pastor or church leader who needs to know the pertinent issues, tested solutions, and real examples of multi-site strategies that are currently being deployed around the world."
>
> — Ed Young, senior pastor, Fellowship Church

"The authors have done their homework. They have firsthand knowledge of the successes and failures of this movement, having been networking with and facilitating dialogue among churches across the country for years."

— Max Lucado, senior minister, Oak Hills Church

"Look no further than this book to propel your ministry to Ephesians 3:20 proportions: exceeding abundantly above all that you could ever ask or think!"

— Randy and Paula White, senior pastors, Without Walls International Church

Softcover: 0-310-27015-4

Pick up a copy today at your favorite bookstore!

The Leadership Network Innovation Series

The Big Idea

Focus the Message, Multiply the Impact

Dave Ferguson, Jon Ferguson, and Eric Bramlett

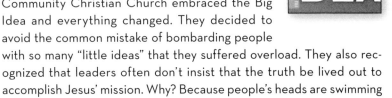

Community Christian Church embraced the Big Idea and everything changed. They decided to avoid the common mistake of bombarding people with so many "little ideas" that they suffered overload. They also recognized that leaders often don't insist that the truth be lived out to accomplish Jesus' mission. Why? Because people's heads are swimming with too many little ideas, far more than they can ever apply.

- *The Big Idea* can help you creatively present one laser-focused theme each week to be discussed in families and small groups.
- *The Big Idea* shows how to engage in a process of creative collaboration that brings people together and maximizes missional impact.
- *The Big Idea* can energize a church staff and bring alignment and focus to many diverse church ministries.

This book shows how the Big Idea has helped Community Christian Church better accomplish the Jesus mission and reach thousands of people in nine locations and launch a church-planting network with partner churches across the country.

This book is part of the Leadership Network Innovation Series.

Softcover: 0-310-27241-6

Pick up a copy today at your favorite bookstore!

Seismic Shifts

The Little Changes That Make a Big Difference in Your Life

Kevin G. Harney

It's easy to talk about changing your life.

Here's how to actually do it.

If you long to experience transformation in the most significant areas of life, this book will become your road map. *Seismic Shifts* is about change — positive, quality change that can help you

- experience deep and lasting joy
- engage in a growing and dynamic relationship with God
- feel healthy, rested, and peaceful
- build intimate relationships marked by honest communication
- attain financial security and contentment
- enjoy sharing your faith naturally and consistently

By making small adjustments in just the right places, you can set off a chain reaction that will redefine the landscape of your life. Dreams really do come true when you learn how to take little steps that make a big difference.

> Small changes can yield huge transformations in the most important areas of your life. My friend Kevin Harney shows you how in his inspiring and practical book.
>
> — Lee Strobel, author, *The Case for Christ* and
> *The Case for a Creator*

> Kevin Harney is both a gifted communicator and a seasoned pastor. *Seismic Shifts* will be a gift to individuals and churches alike.
>
> — John Ortberg, Teaching Pastor, Menlo Park Presbyterian
> Church and author of *God Is Closer Than You Think* and
> *The Life You've Always Wanted*

> Kevin Harney is totally on track with *Seismic Shifts*. With skillful pen, Kevin teaches us how to create powerful movement in our lives.
>
> — Randy Frazee, Teaching Pastor at Willow Creek Community
> Church and author of *The Connecting Church* and
> *Making Room for Life*

Hardcover, Jacketed: 0-310-25945-2

Finding a Church You Can Love and Loving the Church You've Found

Kevin and Sherry Harney

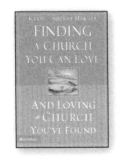

How to Find Your Best Fit

Whether you grew up going to church twice on Sundays or never set foot in a church at all, finding and sinking your roots into a church community is crucial to your spiritual well-being. Finding the right church home can be a huge challenge, and also a lot of fun.

Kevin and Sherry Harney point out that, while no church is perfect, some will fit you better than others. They show what a healthy church looks like, how to handle hot issues facing churches today, and how to determine whether a church's unique worship style will inspire or distract you. Even better, the Harneys help you discover how to plug into a church and experience the joy of giving back.

In the words of the authors, "Church can be one of the most joy-filled, life-giving experiences you will ever have." Practical, encouraging, and true to the Bible, this book is your road map to finding a spiritual community you can really love.

Softcover: 0-310-24679-2

Pick up a copy today at your favorite bookstore!

We want to hear from you. Please send your comments about this book to us in care of zreview@zondervan.com. Thank you.